Pintsized Pioneers at Play

Homemade Frontier Fun and Danger

Preston Lewis

and

Harriet Kocher Lewis

San Angelo, Texas

ISBN: 978-1-964830-11-7
Imprint: Bariso Press

Edited by: Harriet Kocher Lewis

Library of Congress Control Number: 2025917000

Book Two of the Pintsized Pioneers Series

Cover Illustration: DALL-E
Cover Design: Preston Lewis
Printed in the United States of America

With Thanks To

Hannah, Cora, Miriam, Carys and Jackson

For All the Playtime Fun
During Camp Mema/Gulag P-Pa

Bariso Press

Harriet Kocher Lewis
Editor and Publisher

CONTENTS

Introduction   i

1   Little Explorers   1

2   Pets and Beasts   14

3   Fun and Danger   32

4   Playing with Fire   57

5   Santa and Firecrackers   73

6   Big Tops and Footlights   97

7   Books and Bibles   119

8   Mistakes, Mishaps and Mischief   139

9   Toys and Dolls   162

10 Pintsized Play   183

    Acknowledgements   190

    Glossary   193

    For Further Reading   196

    About the Authors   201

Introduction

This book is the sequel to our Spur Award- and Will Rogers Gold Medallion-winning *Pintsized Pioneers: Taming the West, One Chore at a Time*. That book explored the chores and contributions of those generally aged sixteen and younger in settling the frontier, an environment with much work to be done and not enough adults to do it. Consequently, child labor—most often within a family unit— became a necessity not only to make ends meet but also to survive in many cases. No matter how small the children, every little bit they contributed through their chores helped their clan feed, clothe, and shelter themselves. As kids matured, their jobs and assistance toward household success grew until they carried heavy loads that would seem almost abusive by contemporary standards.

Despite the many tasks they handled and the boredom associated with menial and repetitive duties, children were still children with an innate instinct to play whenever they could, wherever they could, however they could. As a result, we decided to examine another aspect of juvenile frontier life by exploring what they did for recreation. Because their labor was such a disruptive part of their young lives, we looked at what they did to amuse themselves. Thus was born *Pintsized Pioneers at Play*.

In determining our research parameters, we gave play a broad definition to encompass most activities beyond their assigned household and outside duties. Further, we defined their schooling as playtime—even though youngsters then and today might disagree, save for periods devoted to recess. Even if attending school wasn't recreation, it was a break from the tedious tasks they dealt with on most days, excepting Sundays, generally reserved as a day of rest and worship.

Simultaneously with the taming of the frontier, pioneers in the field of child psychology were beginning to study the emotional and cognitive development of young children. English naturalist, geologist, and biologist Charles Darwin (1809-1882), is best known for penning the influential 1859 *On the Origin of Species*, but he also conducted one of the first systematic studies of developmental psychology in children. Darwin published in 1877 a short paper detailing the evolution of communication skills in babies, based on scientific observations of his infant son, Doddy.

By the late nineteenth century in the United States, psychologist and educator G. Stanley Hall (1844-1924), who earned the first U.S. doctorate in psychology at Harvard College, was conducting extensive research on the stages of human lifespan development. Today, Hall is considered the "father of child psychology" in the United States. Darwin and Hall provided the psychological foundation for Swiss psychologist Jean Piaget (1896-1980) to outline the phases of cognitive development in children. His work analyzed how children's thinking evolves from the simple to the complex as they grow. Piaget's concepts revolutionized educational theory in teaching youngsters and broadened developmental research into adolescent cognitive maturation.

While *Pintsized Pioneers at Play* is not an examination of childhood psychology, Piaget's stages of childhood intellectual development provide a better understanding of children and their play in a frontier environment. From birth to age sixteen, youngsters progress through four stages of intellectual growth. Gradually, according to Piaget, children begin to understand cause and effect and to grasp the potential consequences of their actions.

From birth to two years, infants learn through sensory experiences and motor activities with only a rudimentary understanding of cause and effect, such as crying brings attention or shaking a rattle produces noise. Infant perceptions of danger are limited, and babies learn only by repeated experience that pulling hair, for instance, hurts. Baby actions like grasping or jiggling objects help develop sensory awareness and motor coordination. During this phase, random babbling becomes more focused, allowing the toddler to communicate with simple words. Play at this age is usually solitary, but crucial in forming the basic mental functions necessary for intellectual growth. Piaget called this the "Sensorimotor Stage."

Piaget's "Preoperational Stage" covered the ages of two to seven when symbolic thinking emerges and language development accelerates. Childhood reasoning during this period remains self-centered, as the youngsters lack the intellectual capacity to understand the perspective of others. While they may learn from adult warnings, they still engage in risky behaviors with little concept of the potential consequences. Play in this phase becomes more imitative, with children copying chores and activities of their parents or other adults.

The ages from seven to eleven produced Piaget's "Concrete Operational Stage," when youths develop logical thinking patterns, and when they better understand cause and effect. Even after they begin to comprehend the perspectives of others, they struggle with abstract thinking. Though they may grasp rules and the concept of danger, they still take risks in new situations or in response to peer pressure. Play remains imitative, but more realistic and often more structured with rules.

Piaget classified the ages from eleven to sixteen as the "Formal Operational Stage," when abstract thinking and hypothetical reasoning develop, providing a greater sense of moral reasoning. Children in this age group can better understand the long-term consequences of their actions and can more accurately weigh potential risks. Though their reasoning is stronger, it doesn't always counter their impulsivity, their susceptibility to peer pressure, or their sense of invincibility. Imitative play becomes more realistic and applicable to real-world situations.

Throughout all four stages, play remains a critical instrument in childhood development, though not all boys and girls mature at the same rate physically, emotionally, or intellectually. Some take more time than others, just as some take longer to learn to read books or solve arithmetic problems.

On its own, the word "play" seems so innocent and harmless, but in a dangerous frontier environment it often turned deadly. Originally, we intended to give the book the subtitle of *Homemade Frontier Fun*. However, as we began our research in culling through newspaper articles from the time, we soon concluded that play in the West produced numerous perils, some associated with the natural naïveté of young children, but many others resulting from the hazardous surroundings in which those youngsters romped and played. As a result, we broadened our subtitle and called this volume *Pintsized Pioneers at Play: Homemade Frontier Fun and Danger*.

This account may represent a skewed view of childhood recreation on the frontier, since newspapers seldom reported on child recreation without injury to the individual or damage to the home or community. Hazards came in many varieties, from animals both wild and domestic, from firearms and matches, and from the tools and implements of miners, farmers, cowhands, and city folks. Of all the chores pioneer children handled, hunting and fishing were the two they enjoyed the most, considering them more fun than work as they provided a break from other more monotonous duties. As those activities were covered in *Pintsized Pioneers*, we have excluded them from this account except for occasional accounts that illustrate the resulting fun or danger.

Most of these stories of play come from history books, diaries, newspaper articles or recollections of those who matured on the frontier. This account, as did its predecessor *Pintsized Pioneers*, relies on the groundbreaking research of Elliott West, who in 1989 published *Growing Up With the Country: Childhood on the Far Western Frontier*, the seminal work on the childhood experience in the pioneering West. As writers, we all stand on the shoulders of those who have preceded us along the trails our writing takes us. Dr. West's shoulders are indeed broad for his many contributions to helping all Americans understand their Old West heritage.

One elegant source on the childhood frontier was Hamlin Garland's *Boy Life on the Prairie,* published in 1899. Garland later admitted the book was more autobiographical than fiction. Thus, whenever *Boy Life on the Prairie* is quoted, it is done with Garland's name rather than that of his fictional counterpart. Otherwise, all names—if they were available—are those of the children or their family members. While Garland was a published author familiar with proper grammar and syntax, not all those cited in the following pages were as well educated. In direct quotes, their words are usually left as they were recorded, even if they included grammatical errors. We did correct spelling mistakes for ease of reading.

Our chapters include Little Explorers on the wonders of the West for children, who often took time to observe the details that their parents missed. A chapter on Pets and Beasts looks at the interplay between youngsters and animals, both wild and domestic. The chapter on Fun and Danger examines innocent recreation like marbles and jump rope as well as some of the imitation games that often produced deadly results. The chapter on Playing with Fire focuses on children's interplay with matches, firearms, and explosives, again with fatal outcomes. Santa and Firecrackers is a chapter looking at the two holidays children most enjoyed in the West. A Big Tops and Footlights section looks at the excitement that circuses and theatrical troupes brought to isolated frontier communities. The Books and Bible section documents the role of the school and church in frontier children's lives and recreation. The chapter on Mistakes, Mishaps, and Mischief shows some of the additional hazards of play from the frontier era. A chapter on Toys and Dolls illustrates typical period playthings, and how their availability changed over the decades. The concluding chapter summarizes Pintsized Play.

Along with *Pintsized Pioneers: Taming the Frontier, One Chore at a Time*, we hope *Pintsized Pioneers at Play: Homemade Frontier Fun and Danger* balances out the frontier experience, giving children their due. In their stories reside lessons for today's youth about the importance of play and how it shaped the nation's pioneer generation. Unfortunately, other lessons about the dangers of Old West play emerge in this study. Those fatal results are often shocking, but are necessary to understand the dangerous environments in which many frontier children lived and played.

Pintsized Pioneers
at Play

Chapter One

Little Explorers

Though born in New York City the son of Italian immigrant parents, little Fiorello Henry La Guardia spent his childhood years on U.S. Army posts from the Dakota Territory to Arizona Territory as his father was a warrant officer and chief musician with the Eleventh Infantry. Years later he wrote of Fort Huachuca, his first army post in Arizona in the late 1880s: "Its location, miles and miles from urban civilization, its barren hills, and bleak surroundings made it exceedingly unpleasant and undesirable for grown-ups, but a paradise for a little boy. We could ride burros. Our playground was not measured in acres or city blocks, but in miles and miles. We could do just about everything a little boy dreams of."

About the same time in 1886, another army brat named Doug MacArthur first attended regular classes at Fort Leavenworth in Kansas, later admitting he was a mediocre pupil at best because of the vast playground presented by his environment. "The freedom and the lure of the West was still in my blood, and I was a poor student."

The daughter of an abusive father who kept her close to home and isolated from her youthful peers in northwestern Nebraska, little Mari Sandoz had fewer chances to explore the countryside than did Fiorello or Doug. Instead, she befriended the Indian children, who often camped with their parents around the Sandoz homestead, and young Mari explored the nuances of their indigenous culture as they played together.

History remembers explorers like frontier scout Kit Carson, who opened numerous trails in the West; mountain man guide Jim Bridger, who explored the Rocky Mountains; and Narcissa Whitman, who as one of the first white women to cross the Rockies helped open the Oregon Trail. But legions of children followed in their pioneering paths, becoming pintsized explorers—little Kit Carsons or Narcissa Whitmans—in their modest slice of the American West.

While the youngsters' discoveries might not have been as momentous as those of Carson, Bridger, or Whitman, they amused themselves with playful findings that their parents had neither the time nor the will to make. After all, the youngsters encountered an entirely new world before them, a world full of natural wonders, amazing animals, and limitless opportunities for play. Certainly, the pioneering experience could be challenging and often dangerous, but the ever-adapting kids always found time and energy for play, something that amazed and even frustrated their parents, especially on the long, tiring journeys across the country.

From 1841 through 1865, approximately forty thousand children made the trek west on the great overland trails from the banks of the Missouri River to the territories bordering the Pacific Ocean. Each year, except for the California Gold Rush years, one of every five immigrants heading toward the setting sun was a child.

On her pioneer journey, little Eliza Donner remembered playing with her dolls and watching the white-covered prairie schooners rolling westward. "During a rest break, we children, who had been confined to the wagon so many hours each day, stretched our limbs, and scampered off on Mayday frolics. We waded the creek, made mud pies, and gathered posies in the narrow glades between the cottonwood, beech, and alder trees."

Fifteen-year-old Mary Eliza Warner, on her 1864 journey, wrote poetry as she journeyed west and in the evenings read her poems to others in the wagon train. She also sketched the dramatic western landscape as her party headed westward. Young Susan Thompson practiced her violin on the journey, and in the evenings she serenaded her fellow travelers.

Many a young girl on the overland trails explored the joys of sewing while confined to a wagon. Their mothers gave them little baskets or bags filled with scraps of cloth, needles, thread, and a thimble so they could pass their time stitching cloth together for doll clothing and learning the rudiments of stitchery and sewing. Andrietta Applegate was one such young seamstress who amused herself that way during her 1851 journey to Oregon. The activity helped time fly on the long journey and left Andrietta with a useful skill once her family reached their destination.

At stops along the trail, many boys and girls knocked over anthills or dug up ant beds looking for beads dropped by Indians during their nomadic travels. It seemed that ants collected the lost beads in their dens and young children took joy in gathering them from the ant beds, provided they avoided insect stings.

As a girl growing up in 1860s Texas, Sarah Harkey Hall remembered being both frightened and curious about the Comanche that traversed the country. She feared being abducted by the Indians and remained nervous when they were near. Yet once they departed, it was a different matter and an opportunity to explore their abandoned camps for playthings. "We would often venture out to the old vacated wigwams to gather trinkets left by the Indians, beads and such like. We always had strand after strand of them, which our childish hearts enjoyed. Although once we were missed by our parents, we would hear the call, 'Come here, children, you will be picked up by the Indians,' then we would take to our heels."

Seventeen-year-old Sarah Ide, who traveled west with her parents to California, at her journey's end remembered the trek fondly. "To me the journey was a pleasure trip, so many beautiful wild flowers, such wild scenery, mountains, rocks, and streams—something new at every turn, or at least every day!" Sarah saw beauty in what her parents may well have seen as obstacles to reaching the promised land of their intended destination.

Sarah's curiosity on the natural wonders on the journey westward was reflected by other youngsters, even after they settled in their new homes. Through their curiosity, they took the time to explore the flora and fauna, some making notes about it in their diaries or journals. While their parents focused on exploiting the land to survive, their sons and daughters explored the terrain, as children are apt to do.

As they investigated along the trail or around their new homes, the young ones collected everything from insects to snakeskins and from bones to lizards. Some kids even gathered animal dung, not just for fuel in the West's woodless areas, but also to amuse themselves in trying to determine which animals had produced the droppings. They discovered that rabbits and hares left petite round pellets while buffalo deposited a ringed, tubular scat four or more inches in length, compared to the inch-long, capsule shaped dregs of the antelope.

A pioneering child in Sheridan County, Nebraska, in the 1880s and 1890s, Charley O'Kieffe assessed the relative merits of cow patties and buffalo chips, comparing them to matzo and Swedish health bread. Children acquired this knowledge by observation, just as the mountain men and trappers of the early frontier had used such information to track animals for food, hides, and pelts.

Young O'Kieffe, perhaps because of his prairie isolation and loneliness, came to view the plants and animals almost as people, ascribing personalities to flora like the tumbleweed and Nebraska Sandhills' fruit-bearing sand cherry shrub. He also gave human characteristics to mammals such as the region's numerous gophers and to birds like the bobolinks common to the plains.

In Kansas, newly arrived Luna Warner gathered and studied a hundred and seventeen plants she discovered around her family's new homestead, cataloging them and noting their individual characteristics. Further north in Montana, little Lillian Miller grew fascinated by the variety of birds in the region. She documented in her journal the coloration patterns of various species, including thrushes, swallows, finches, and curlews. Lillian learned to imitate the calls of dozens of wild birds in addition to those of the chickens her family kept. In Iowa, young Ellison Orr studied the flying and feeding habits of numerous birds, such as cowlinks, grouse, partridges, pigeons, quails, and shrikes.

Frank Waugh, who at four arrived in Kansas with his parents, loved the land and studied its plants and animals as a boy, learning to describe such things as the differences—other than height—between the big and little bluestem grasses of the prairie and the subtleties of plains plants such as the buffalo pea, flowering thistle, milk weed, rattle weed, and wild aster. As a young boy, Waugh found it disheartening that some of his adult neighbors could identify only the sunflower and the cocklebur among the hundreds of plants on the prairie. As he described their ignorance in his memoirs, "the stars above and weeds underfoot were equally nameless and therefore insignificant. Every wild plant was a weed. All wild plants, like all wild animals, had to be destroyed to make way for farms."

Beyond the rural areas, town children explored their urban environments. As a kid in Virginia City, Nevada, John Taylor Waldorf remembered exploring the fire-blackened ruins of a Virginia City shanty, looking for something to play with. When the irate owner confronted him, young Waldorf got his "first peep into the barrel of a revolver ... [that] looked like a cannon to me." Deciding the distraught owner did not care to play with him anymore than John now desired to play in the remains of his home, Waldorf escaped. Years later, he recalled, "As far as I know, I still hold the white ten-year-old championship record for climbing close-boarded, seven foot-fences."

Young Waldorf also explored under his Virginia City house, digging with his friends beneath the place in search of the buried treasure a local seeress had informed his mother was hidden under their dwelling. By the time he finished exploring, he had excavated a cellar. "I can still recall my blistered hands, but I have no regrets because for days I spent imaginary millions and was richer then than I have ever been since," he wrote years later. Waldorf never learned if the claim was true or merely a ruse to get him and his pals to dig the cellar.

A Montana girl growing up in Deer Lodge Valley recalled her girlhood days and adventures. As Ella Irvine Mountjoy remembered it, "From early March, when the snow was disappearing and the first flowers beginning to bloom, until October, when the hardiest fall flowers and the autumn leaves covered the mountainside with treasures, I with my brothers and sisters roamed the mountains and hills and explored the streams for miles in every direction."

Young west Texan Ralla Banta and her siblings were tasked with herding the family's flock of sheep. "When we returned home in the evening," she recalled, "we enjoyed telling where we had been, to what creek, up what branch, and what we had seen."

In Montana and elsewhere throughout the West stood natural wonders aplenty, from the smallest colored pebbles to gather to the house-sized boulders to climb. In places fossils poked through the earth just waiting for a child to find and ponder. Prairie dogs skittered around, tempting boys to give chase, and wildflowers waved in the breeze, inviting girls to pick them. There for the taking were pottery shards and arrowheads left behind by the Indians who had preceded them.

Youth Edwin Lewis Bennett collected dozens of arrow points in the hills around his Creede, Colorado, home. "We found arrowheads everywhere, so numerous we wouldn't think of taking in a defective one. If it was not practically perfect, we threw it back and looked for a better one. We might as well have left them all out on the hill, for we gave them away to anyone who wanted them. Judging by the arrowheads, thousands of Indians must have occupied that area for hundreds of years."

Thirteen-year-old John Norton's Kansas family homestead stood near Fort Larned (1859-1878) where young John and his brothers scoured the post's perimeter, searching for unspent bullets at the target range and other trophies at the installation's garbage dump. They discovered more expended shells than live ammunition, but their explorations over time included such trophies as two pieces of petrified wood, a battered canteen, a bugler's badge, and a zinc collar pad used on harnesses for horses.

Silverton, Oregon, children playing along Silver Creek in 1886 found a piece of gold-bearing rock in the streambed and, according to newspaper reports, "now there is a gold craze among the inhabitants of the little city."

Boys playing around an old culvert outside Pleasantville, Iowa, discovered "a robbers' den," according to newspaper accounts. Their juvenile haul produced a basket of watches, chains, jewelry, silverware, and money but found "no trace of the robbers." The newspaper reported "the property has nearly all been returned to owners in various parts of the country."

Boys exploring among the willow trees near the Kirk ranch outside of San Jose, California, in 1871, discovered a partially buried iron safe. After uncovering and opening it, the playmates discovered papers identifying the container as the property of Donald McKenzie and his local iron foundry. The safe had been pilfered three years earlier.

In an article headlined "Betrayed by Boys," a Nebraska newspaper reported on Fremont youngsters playing near an old beer vault and finding one of the "gold watches stolen from Pratt's jewelry store" two weeks earlier. After the kids reported the find to authorities, the sheriff and chief of police staked out the place and captured Leonard Healy and Thomas Francis. "Both are hard cases," reported the *Omaha World-Herald*, "and if not the two who robbed Pratt, must be wanted somewhere else."

Some boys exploring a Davenport, Iowa, lumberyard in 1884 unearthed a container with "several pounds of counterfeit ten-cent pieces, bearing the date of 1844."

In Orange, Texas, the easternmost city in the Lone Star State, lads playing near a railroad bridge found clothing and shoes hidden under the trestlework. The young ones carried their find to local police officers who connected them to the previous night's burglary of W. Bluestein's store. Suspicions fell on John Elias, a painter recently arrived in town from Michigan. The clothes were valued at twenty dollars. When Elias could not make the ten-dollar bail, he was jailed.

In 1896 Oakesdale, Washington, a handful of boys exploring under a local warehouse discovered a dry-goods box filled with boys' suits, shoes, straw hats, and jewelry, all property of a local general merchandise firm that had been a victim of petty thievery for months. The stolen goods were returned to the store, though the thieves remained unidentified.

Young boys playing on a canal bank near Retford, Kansas, found a hole full of silver coins in April 1890. The *Wichita Weekly Beacon* reported, "Nine of the lads filled their caps with the money, which they took to the police station." The paper continued, "The treasure place was afterward thoroughly searched, and altogether two-hundred-and-fifty-dollars' worth of coins were taken out. The coins had evidently been under ground for many years."

In 1896 Wharton, Texas, several boys playing in the sand by the Colorado River found a buried cache of silver coins valued at sixty-seven dollars. The *Fort Worth Daily Gazette* failed to report if the youngsters got to split their find among themselves.

Discoveries were not always benign or rewarding. Two girls playing on a Portland, Oregon, wharf in 1897 saw a blob in the water and picked it up. To their horror, it was the severed head of another girl. Terrified at the discovery, the girls on the wharf tossed the head back into the Willamette River and notified the police, who found two cut braids of hair near the wharf. The police initiated a search for the missing body part. Noted the newspaper, "There is a tragedy, doubtless, back of the matter."

Two Oklahoma boys playing on the outskirts of Chandler came across the remnants of a large campfire and began poking around in the ashes, only to discover a human skull. Reported the *Austin Weekly Statesman*, "They did not wait for further examination but hurried to town and told what they had found." Men responding to the news rushed to the site and discovered portions of three legs, two heads, and four arms, but not enough to identify the deceased or even their gender. The grand jury investigating the crime ruled a verdict of "death of two unknown persons by means unknown."

In Deadwood, Dakota Territory, two young males exploring the mountainsides east of town discovered a man's body with a bullet through the head. "From all appearances, the man has evidently been murdered in cold blood and robbed," reported the *Deseret News* in Salt Lake City. A memorandum book removed from the man bore the name of Charles E. Lee, who had arrived in the mining boomtown within the week.

From Guthrie, Oklahoma Territory, in late August of 1892, came a dispatch of two boys playing in the woods near Beaver in the Oklahoma Panhandle. They found "clothes containing the skeleton of their unfortunate owner" with a bullet hole in the skull, reported the *Minco Minstrel*. By his clothes, the victim was identified as O.K. Rogers, a hardware merchant and the city clerk of Beaver. The fellow was last seen in town one night the previous January "with a large amount of money in his possession."

A Sunday afternoon game of hide-and-seek discovered something the Kansas boys were not prepared for in an oat bin in a livery stable owned by Henry Schaffer, a onetime barber who had begun studying medicine. One boy slipped into the stable and crawled into the oat bin, trying to hide under a gunnysack. "As he raised the sack," reported the *Wichita Star*, "he was horrified to find that he had crawled in on top of a skeleton to the bones of which some of the flesh still adhered." The accidental explorer "fled screaming from the scene and soon the whole neighborhood was aroused and flocked to the scene of the discovery."

The ensuing investigation by the Wichita coroner and sheriff revealed that the bones were the property of a medical student and had been used in a med school dissection. After the dissection, the medical students threw dice to determine who would take the remains. Stable owner and medical student Schaffer won the dubious prize and decided to store the skeleton in the stable for safekeeping.

Concluded the *Star*, "The neighbors are highly indignant and demand that the skeleton be taken away and properly buried. They do not care to have human remains lying thus loosely around, so that their children can find them in their play, and assert that the matter will be closely investigated."

Period newspapers document dozens of instances of children playing and finding the bodies of dead babies. In 1870 youngsters playing at Front and P streets in Gold Hill, Nevada, found a carpet sack which they opened to discover a dead male baby "quite large and well-formed, and appeared to be an infant of which its father and mother might be proud, instead of harboring murderous thoughts against it," commented the town's *Daily News*.

Children playing in an Albuquerque alley in 1887 discovered a tiny foot protruding from an ash heap and discovered a baby described by the *Albuquerque Journal* as "a well-formed child, which, although perfect in every limb and feature, had evidently remained in the world no longer than to breathe a few feeble gasps of life. Its little head was covered with a silken mass of dark, curling hair, and its features bore the placid smile of sleeping innocence."

Other instances included boys playing on the banks of the North Concho River near San Angelo, Texas, in 1891 discovering a bundle, which when unraveled exposed a newborn baby with the back of its skull crushed; and other boys near Houston's old Fair Grounds addition finding a bunch of corn sacks hiding the remains of an infant. This was a too common discovery in frontier communities.

A less grisly discovery was made on an 1899 Sunday afternoon, when boys playing under a street bridge in Salem, Oregon, found a pile of convict clothing, which they turned over to Police Chief D.W. Gibson. The prison uniform was identified as belonging to a recent escapee named "Richardson," who left "his confined quarters" earlier in the week. Though his clothes were discovered, the wearer was not, and the police continued their search.

Because frontier children were adept at riding horses, their mounts could take them far afield for explorations great distances from their homes. "I learned to ride hosses so well that by the time I was six, I could ride a running hoss barebacked," recalled W.H. Childers, who was born in 1866 in Wood County, Texas, and grew up there and in Cooke County. "In fact, I never had a real saddle until I was fourteen years old."

Hamlin Garland remembered he and his Iowa buddies "lived in the saddle when no other duties called ... and the world seemed a very good place for a boy."

Growing up in Taos, New Mexico Territory, young Lorin Brown recalled how he and his boy playmates were fascinated with horses. "My peers and I knew every horse in the vicinity, from the saddle horses, to the harnessed ones ... to those used by the freighters. It was no wonder that in our play we emulated horses."

On army posts where children were more numerous and chores fewer than on homesteads, riding was a favored recreation among the youngsters and their mothers. Army brats Jack and David Biddle learned to ride when they were only four years old. Astride their ponies, Jack and

David could explore the countryside or imitate their soldier father.

For young Edwin Lewis Bennett and his playmates, the mounts of choice in the mining community of Creede, Colorado, were donkeys. "Every kid had a burro and some of them had two," Bennett remembered. "Burros grazed all over town and out in the hills, and it was not unusual for us to spend more time roaming the hills in search of our mounts than we did riding after we found them."

Horses helped children overcome the limitations of distance and explore places far beyond their homes. Further, their mounts offered the young equestrians another outlet for entertainment. A young girl among the Forty-niners remembered, "I was a fearless rider, and nothing pleased me more than to be mounted on a swift horse." Atop their favorite steeds, pintsized riders chased antelopes and coyotes, one west Texas girl claiming to have pursued a coyote almost fifty-five miles one Thanksgiving Day without ever catching her prey. After a similar but equally unsuccessful chase of a Kansas coyote, Luna Warner acknowledged to her diary the failure to capture her quarry, but added, "Wasn't it fun, though?"

Another fun amusement popular among children as well as adults was horse racing. Kids often raced their mounts—both horses and donkeys—in formal and informal matches. Horses remained an essential part of frontier life and broadened the range of pintsized pioneer explorations. Other animals, both domesticated and wild, provided opportunities for fun and danger as well.

Chapter Two

Pets and Beasts

nimals on the American frontier were both a blessing and a curse—pets and beasts—to the children who lived in the West. For pintsized pioneers, domesticated animals became more than just pets, serving not only as cherished companions but also as needed protectors in a rugged and dangerous environment. The wild animals roaming the region remained potential threats of injury and death to children. These "beasts" ranged from rattlesnakes to wildcats to wolves to bears and even to some domesticated animals that went mad with rabies. Despite those potential dangers from wild or rabid animals, children maintained fond memories of the many animals that were a part of their daily lives.

As an only child, one northern California girl remembered no one to play with at home, "only myself and cows and the dogs and the chickens." She recalled her mother providing her dolls to play with and instructing her to pretend she was keeping house. Remembered the girl years later, "So I took the dolls out to the shed and sat them down in chairs and tried to talk to them, but they didn't talk back. The chickens were lots more fun."

Horses were so essential to frontier life that children who had no pony to ride or pull their toy wagons would harness the family dog or a goat to their homemade carts and organize mock parades about the farm, showing off for the other barnyard animals.

With the spring birthing season, farm and ranch children welcomed new colts and calves. "How we would pet them and spoil them," recalled Stephanie Prepiora of her North Dakota homestead childhood with her brothers and sisters. "There were baby chicks, turkeys, ducks, and geese, all requiring work, but it was a work of love and all pleasures." Twelve-year-old Mary Rebecca Williams of Homer, Iowa, wrote to her older brother working in Georgia in 1860 of the new calves and the names she had given them. Little Rebecca said the "largest is Marmy Duke. Prince Albert. Queen Victoria. Princess Adalade. Hatty. Cupid. Old Brunts calf [we call] Moon, because he has such big eyes."

Returning from her Greene County, Missouri, school one day, Martha Gay found an orphaned lamb and brought it home. She was delighted when her parents allowed her to keep the animal, which she pampered and played with for months. "We had many a romp with our lamb," she recalled, but when the orphan matured into a ram, he attacked her younger brother. Martha intervened to save her sibling from more serious injury. Shortly after that, her father took the ram to market for slaughter, and Martha was "not sorry to see him go."

On the plains of eastern Montana, Urma DeLong Taylor rescued a chick with his legs tangled in a wad of horsehair and adopted him as her own special pet. She pampered "Pete" to maturity, making him in her words "a spoiled child" that she kept in the house, "even allowing him to perch on the family sugar bowl."

Children on prairie farms had plenty of small animals to play with. Young Myrtle Lobdell recalled her joyous early memories of childhood. "My very first memory is of chasing a pet duck about on a sunny hillside, the 'quack, quack' with which he would elude my outstretched hands when I pursued him, and the happy way he would come and settle himself in my lap or by my side at other times. I have thought of that duck many times in later years, when I have seen a thing or person too urgently pursued." Myrtle also remembered "a family of playful kittens romping like squirrels over the branches of a fallen tree that had been dragged from the wooded stream nearby for fuel."

Of her youth, Clara M. Barber remembered problems with mice during her childhood and a tough decision she had to make one day. When her father went to town, she always asked him to buy her a nickel's worth of candy, but on this occasion, he inquired whether she would rather have the sweet treat or a mousetrap. "I hesitated, for I knew we needed the mousetrap, but finally decided he should get it. When he came home and handed me the trap, I knew I would have to do without candy for some time, for the trap had cost fifteen cents. The trap worked all right and before we retired that evening, we had caught twenty-four mice."

In addition to mice, dangerous rattlesnakes crawled everywhere. Prairie girl Bessie Wilson remembered fetching a board on which to make her mud pies one day. As soon as she moved the piece of wood, a rattlesnake poked out of a hole. "It raised its head about five or six inches and began lolling its long red tongue at me. I was too young to be frightened but called, 'Oh, Mamma! Come and see the snake.' She came running, catching me by the arm and ruthlessly snatching me from my perilous position. By the time she had finished killing this snake with the garden hoe, she was ready to collapse."

Besides riding burros around Creede, Colorado, Edwin Lewis Bennett and his friends watched them a lot for entertainment. He remembered one coming out of a cluttered alley with a mail-order catalog in his mouth. The donkey dropped the volume in the middle of the street, placed a hoof on it and licked up a page, tearing it from its nest and eating the catalog page by page. As Bennett told it, "Leaf by leaf, he worked his way through the children's clothes, ladies underwear, hats, boots, and men's suits. But when he came to the machinery and tool section, he lifted his foot for the last time on that catalog and ambled off up the street, leaving us to wonder if he figured out all that steel was too much even for a burro's digestive equipment."

Texas daughter Frances Bramlette Farris got to know legendary Texas Ranger and Indian fighter Bigfoot Wallace, who showed a fondness for young Frances. She later recalled, "It didn't take him long to find out that I was extremely fond of pets. The other children liked them, too, but didn't just live with them as I did, spending most of my time playing with and petting them. He never failed to bring me every young rabbit, squirrel, or anything else he came across—even to a javelina pig and a small black bear."

Francis possessed a particular fondness for the black bear. "That bear was the cutest thing. We had to keep it chained to a tree in the yard, and it had a habit of walking just half way around the tree where it would turn a somersault, walk back to the starting point, turn another somersault, and start over, keeping that up for half a day at a time. Cubby wouldn't let anyone come near him but me, and I loved him very early. Such shrieking and sobbing and carrying on as arose when he died was never heard before. One night some lobo wolves came into the yard and killed him. My poor little Cubby! … No pet I ever had could take the place of Cubby."

As the daughter of an Army officer, Forrestine C. Hooker traveled throughout the West from posts in Oklahoma to Texas to Arizona and loved pets of all types. Over the years, her menagerie included baby mice; two canaries; dozens of horned toads; a pigeon, at least briefly; a white cur pup she named "Prince;" and a big black dog she called "Spy."

Spy was a bit of a troublemaker, who fell out of favor with a family the Hookers resided with in the post officer's quarters. The wife was cooking a steak on the stove and went to tell her husband it would be ready shortly. When she returned, the pan remained atop the stove, but the meat was gone. Only later, when the chaplain reported seeing Spy running off with a steak in his mouth, was the mystery solved. Spy, though, did not return home until well past sunset, having taken a nap after his tasty lunch.

During a family journey between Kansas military posts, Forrestine's father caught a wild pigeon, which he gave his daughter. "He attached a light cord to one of its legs, allowing a string about six feet with a small loop. This he slipped over my finger as I sat in the ambulance. 'Shut your hand tightly,' he said, 'then you can watch the pigeon fly as we drive.'" Everything went fine until she slid the loop from her finger and loosened her grip on the bird.

"There was," she recalled, "a flap, a flash of wings, and my pigeon darted on its way, taking the string with it, while I sat crying. I always regretted losing that pigeon because the string was still tied to its leg when it disappeared from our sight."

In February 1884 the *Arizona Weekly Citizen* in Tucson noted "tin pans and dogs are seldom voluntary company," referring to the practice of "tin-panning" where a mischievous lad tied a baking tin to a mutt's tail and started him on a terrified run. While a common male juvenile prank, tin-panning by girls was indeed news in the paper's opinion. The intrepid reporter noted, "A lot of little girls playing in the Court House Plaza tin-panned a dog that, for about fifty yards to say the least, ran well. Possibly, he had been biting their dolls, so they gave him the tin pan to take home." The girls ranged in age from "little toddlers" to no more than eight years old, according to the paper. As for the dog, the paper reported "the little fellow yelled at every jump, but asked no questions as he went along." Once the terrified dog dashed away, his female tormentors "crowded together like a lot of scared sheep, but as soon as the tail hold [on the tin pan] slipped, they clapped their hands and jumped for joy."

"As long as a boy is a boy, he never loses the desire to own a dog.... It is a sad day to the boy when his mother first conceives the dreadful suspicion that that dog has fleas," according to an 1875 *Sacramento Bee* article.

A boy playing with his dog by the creek where his fishing pole and line had barely drawn a nibble the entire afternoon was greeted by a passing adult. "Nice dog you have there. What's his name?"

"Fish," replied the boy.

"Fish? That's an odd name for a dog. Why do you call him that?"

" 'cause he won't bite."

At the height of the silver boom in Virginia City, Nevada, in late October 1865, a three-year-old Rusk boy and his beloved Newfoundland pup failed to return home after playing all afternoon in the frenetic mining town. John Rusk, the boy's father, notified authorities and the town crier circled the community, ringing his bell and notifying citizens of the missing child. With hundreds of tunnels, mineshafts, and other hazards, police feared the worst, that the boy had stumbled into an open mineshaft.

Twenty-four hours passed without a sign of the two, magnifying worries that the pair had fallen to their deaths in an uncovered mineshaft.

After a fruitless day and night of searching, the boy's exhausted father checked out a tunnel where his son might have wandered behind the town's massive Ophir mine. A hundred and fifty feet from the tunnel's mouth, Rusk came to a hundred-and-thirty-foot-deep shaft in the tunnel floor. As the newspaper described it, "With a faint, indefinite hope that his boy might yet be found, he shouted down the shaft as he had done so many others in his weary search and, to his indescribable joy, a little voice answered from the depths, 'Oh, Pa!'" The lost was found.

The father dashed for help and soon a throng of men arrived to retrieve the lost boy from the bowels of the earth. One man was lowered down with a rope and retrieved the Rusk child, then returned to save the puppy. The boy suffered a badly bruised face, closed left eye, cut upper lip, and swollen and bruised left knee. The pup was slightly bruised, but otherwise fine.

Authorities speculated the boy was holding the canine when he tumbled down the shaft and that the dog cushioned his fall in the damp shaft bottom. Concluded the paper, "We never expect to hear of such a wonderful escape from violent death again," thanks to the Newfoundland pup.

One day shortly after his family arrived in the Cherokee Strip, eight-year-old David Siceloff and his dog were out exploring when Trim spotted his first prairie dog and chased him to a hole where the rodent disappeared. Trim then ran from hole to hole whenever a prairie dog poked his head out and barked at each sentinel. Trim never caught a prairie dog, though he got his nose bit from sticking it into their dens.

Another time Siceloff and a friend were herding the milk cow home when they spotted "a small dirt-colored animal ... flattish [and] nearly as wide as long and covered with short stubby spikes. Its head was covered with hornlike spines." They wanted to catch the lizard, but feared it might be poisonous, especially after blood spurted out of his eyes. Still, they caught him and carried him home where they learned the reptile was a horned toad, the first they had ever seen.

Siceloff recalled that burrowing owls would occupy abandoned prairie dog dens. He and his friends knew owls couldn't turn their eyes, so they twisted their heads instead to see around them. "We were told," he recalled, "if we went round and round [him], he would twist his neck in two. We didn't believe it, but we tried it anyway. It didn't work."

Besides prairie dogs, striped ground squirrels were common on the plains and young Siceloff devised a method of capturing them. He took a twelve-foot length of twine, made a loop in it and placed it over the opening to the ground squirrel's den. Then he hid about ten feet behind the den. When the rodent peeked outside to see if the threat had disappeared, Siceloff would yank the twine and snag the squirrel around the neck. He kept one ground squirrel for a pet and secured him to a piece of lumber, but a "strange bony dog" came by and ate him.

Normally, dogs were man's best friend, but that could change during dry summers when they might catch rabies and turn mad, attacking humans and infecting them with their bites. In those months stray dogs were shot on sight, and men never left the house without a weapon, whether a gun, a pitchfork, or something else. Siceloff recalled, "We boys were told to stay inside the picket fence and if a dog showed up, to get into the house or barn or climb a tree, and be quick about it."

Unlike dogs, coyotes were never man's best friends. Instead, they were a pest, killing chickens and baby calves, lambs, and pigs. Trapping the wary coyote was ineffective, so pioneers turned to poison in Oklahoma and other places. Sometimes it worked on coyotes, and sometimes it had unintended results like Siceloff's dog dying from poison.

Then there were the beastly animals that threatened children during their play, sometimes because of the youngster's own actions. For instance, near Guthrie, Oklahoma, in 1890, a passel of boys were playing with a snapping turtle, holding it up at their faces and annoying it. One young lad stuck out his tongue, as the *Guthrie Democrat* reported, "to see if it would bite." It did. As the newspaper described the aftermath, "The turtle promptly carried out its part of the program, it being found necessary to forcibly remove its hold from the lad's tongue, which was quite severely bitten."

Some attacks were unprovoked. Two Walnut Creek, Arizona, siblings, ages ten and eight, were playing in their yard on a June 1888 morning when a vicious wildcat attacked them while their father was away and their mother was in the house. The woman drove the vicious animal away, but she remained terrified the wildcat might return. When her husband came home, she persuaded him to stay around the house that afternoon. Mom's instincts were right as the animal returned. Her husband grabbed his shotgun to dispatch the animal. Once outside, he lifted his weapon, but the wildcat lunged at him, and he used the shotgun as a club to fend off the infuriated animal, which retreated under the house. The man then pulled his six-shooter and killed the feline, described by the paper as "an immense big cat, and its viciousness can only be accounted for on account of hunger." The newspaper reported the two children's wounds were treated in Prescott and not considered life-threatening.

By contrast, school children playing in a field outside Dillon, Montana, in 1895 startled another wildcat, but scared it so much that it sought safety in a tree.

In Paris, Texas, in 1891, an infuriated cow bolted through the yard and into the James Given house, then charged through the dwelling all the way to the covered back porch where three children were playing. The enraged bovine lunged at the trio, impaling an eleven-year-old boy with her horn just above the groin and "tearing a fearful gash" in the youth's stomach before being driven off.

Samuel Davenport's two sons, ages ten and eight, were frolicking outside in Ogden, Utah, when "the king of birds" swooped down on them and aimed his talons at one boy's head. The eagle's claws snared the youngster's hat instead of his head, sparing him from a serious injury. Finally, the brothers drove the eagle away, but the *Ogden Standard-Examiner* failed to report if they had saved the boy's hat.

The *Canal City Dispatch* in Arkansas City, Kansas, reported that on July 4, 1888, B.R. Bittle had spotted a rabid dog attacking and biting cattle he was overseeing outside of town. Having nothing to shoot the dog with, he chased him off, but the canine headed towards the city. Bittle ran ahead of him to chase kids playing in the road out of danger, but the mad dog kept biting other dogs and animals. When the crazed animal attempted to bite a little child of Charley Combs, Mrs. H.W. Stewart stabbed him with a pair of scissors and saved the child. Once Bittle secured a gun, he shot the rabid animal and ended the immediate danger. In assessing the situation, the *Dispatch* noted, "There is no doubt but that many animals have been bitten by the dog killed by Mr. Bittle, and they will, of course, go mad. It is necessary, therefore, for the people to kill all animals that have been bitten by this dog or kill them when they show the first signs of hydrophobia."

In Little Rock, Arkansas, as late as October 1897, a wolf was killed on Arch Street, one of the town's principal residential thoroughfares, just as it was about to attack a group of neighborhood children playing outside.

Late one October 1885 afternoon in Sherman, Texas, a bear attacked a little girl. This was not, in theory, a wild bear as it was chained behind Crookford's saloon, where several children were teasing the animal. Nine-year-old Mary Meisner annoyed him so much that in one of his furious lunges he snapped the collar around his neck and attacked the girl, chomping her shoulder. A nearby pedestrian, Pramier Frazier, heard the girl's screams, beat the bear off with an iron bar and drove him into an outhouse.

The bear's owner slammed the door shut, retrieved his pistol and fired through the door into the animal, further enraging the furry mammal. As the *Galveston Daily News* reported the incident, "His bearship tore down the door, and his advent caused the numerous bystanders to take [to the] fence-tops. A fusillade was opened on him, and he was killed after fifty shots were fired at him."

Little Mary sustained serious injuries in the attack, "her shoulders being badly chewed, besides two wounds on the back." The paper credited Frazier with rescuing Mary "as when he got to her the bear was chewing away at the child's shoulder and trying to hug the life out of her."

Near Yuma, Arizona, children playing on the bank of an inlet in the Colorado River valley near dairyman J.M. Morales' place spotted something in the water they at first took to be a log. When they saw it moving and with eyes atop the ripples, they raced home to tell their father. Morales grabbed his shotgun, and on reaching the site, "saw in the middle of the stream an animal about ten or twelve feet in length and from the description he gave there is no question but what it was an alligator."

Though he shot at the reptile, it swam away, and Morales journeyed to Yuma to purchase several boxes of cartridges, as "he is afraid it will kill some members of his family." The sighting confirmed similar reports from Mexicans and Indians upriver of "a strange and unknown animal." The newspaper speculated that the alien species was an alligator brought from New Orleans years earlier by the proprietor of the Southern Pacific Hotel. He kept the reptile in a tank until it escaped one night. "It is the opinion of the old-timers that what Mr. Morales has seen is the same one that escaped at that time."

While alligators may have been rare in the Old West, cats and dogs were plentiful and offered furry companionship and even protection. A loyal dog could be a boy's best friend, and a cat might be a girl's "baby" to care for, but the animals also looked after their young human charges.

Around the turn of the century, the ten-year-old daughter of Thomas Lewis, a Sweet Home, Oregon, resident, was returning to the house with a sack of borrowed flour from a neighbor's house a mile away through the woods. She and her little dog startled a cougar that charged them both. According to newspaper accounts, "The dog did brave work in her protection, and succeeded in keeping the ferocious animal off until she reached home." Once she scurried inside and reported the incident, her older brother grabbed his rifle and sent another larger dog after the big cat. When the dog treed the mountain lion, the boy shot him. The predator measured nine feet long from his nose to the tip of his tail.

About the same time in St. Louis, Missouri, a family collie saved a five-year-old city boy named Arthur Loeb by dragging the child from the streetcar tracks "just in time to prevent his life being crushed out by an electric car," according to newspaper reports. The rescue was the second instance within the previous four months that the dog had snatched little Arthur from the rails before a streetcar passed, reported the local paper.

In Stanton County, Kansas, three-year-old Marie Lyman was playing near a haystack with her dog when an eagle swooped down and tried to snatch her. Hearing the commotion at the pile of hay, Marie's father, J.C. Lyman, grabbed a club and raced toward the noise. He found the dog named "Nero" battling the eagle until the bird knocked the dog senseless with its powerful wings. Lyman battered the bird to death and saved his terrified daughter. The eagle measured six feet across from wingtip to wingtip.

A shepherd dog belonging to Fred Balz, Jr., of Freemont, Nebraska, saved the life of his master's two-and-a-half-year-old son, who disappeared for nineteen hours in a rainstorm. With the dog as his companion, the toddler wandered away from home in the evening. When his parents failed to locate their boy, they sought the help of neighbors to find him, but a heavy rainstorm slowed their efforts and increased their concern for the child's safety.

Throughout the long night of strong winds and intermittent deluges, searchers tramped woods and fields waving lanterns and calling for the boy. Nineteen hours after he disappeared, the volunteers found the toddler sheltered behind a large rock near a creek bank, where the dog had dragged him. Living up to the reputation of his breed, the dog stood like a shepherd over his little charge. Though wet from the storm, the child was otherwise unharmed, thanks to the family pooch.

In 1899, two California newspapers reported on a twelve-year-old bulldog named "McGinty" that belonged to a fireman. McGinty was outside when he saw little Mattie Williams doing chores nearby when her dress caught fire. The bulldog rushed to the small girl's aid, tearing her flaming clothes from her body with his teeth. McGinty saved the lass's life, with the tiny mistress receiving only minor burns. Mattie's mother said her daughter "would have been cremated had it not been for the dog."

Another canine not belonging to the family made one of the most dramatic rescues on record in 1890 in San Francisco Bay. "Nep" was a mascot for the steamer *Tiburon* when he was napping on a wharf in the bay while a family was fishing about fifty yards away. When one of the family hooked a fish, a three-year-old tot slipped and tumbled off the landing into the water. The excitement roused Nep, who raced down the wharf, and leaped into the water before any of the adult men could react. According to news reports, "Like a flash, 'Nep' went head first off the high wharf into the water. The little one was not ten feet away, and in a moment he had a piece of the child's clothing in his mouth. He turned to shore, and before the men in the party could get their coats off, the dog had landed the baby safe and sound." A grateful mother hugged both her baby and the rescuer, then offered to buy the canine from its owner, who was too fond of his hero dog to sell him.

When Sam Dodge of Montgomery County, Kansas, left his ranch on a trip south into Indian Territory, he never realized his five-year-old daughter Bessie with the family's Newfoundland dog at her side had followed him. When the child's mother realized Bessie was missing, she frantically notified the neighbors. A desperate search ensued. Not until the next day and ten miles away did the searchers find Bessie still being protected by the torn and bleeding dog. At the Newfoundland's feet lay two dead wolves the dog had fought off to protect the child. The following day, after the child and dog returned home, the canine died from his wounds. The grateful father purchased a granite monument to place at the head of the dog's grave.

Family cats could be heroes as well, helping save life and property. In 1875 Sherman, Texas, Tom Ed Bomar watched his three-year-old son walk down a narrow weed-and-grass-lined pathway with their playful house cat at his side. Suddenly, the cat lunged at something about three feet in front of Bomar's son. Rushing to see the cause of the commotion, the horrified father spotted the cat battling a large rattlesnake coiled in front of the child. While his bemused and confused son stood clapping his hands with excitement, Bomar killed the rattler, then tended his cat, which was bitten in several places, but survived the encounter.

During a Monday morning breakfast at the Bell County, Texas, home of Will Moore and his family, the diners heard the strange cries of their house cat from the front room. When Moore's young son went to investigate, he found a small blaze inside. The cat's woeful warning provided enough time for the family to alert neighbors and extinguish the fire before the house was totally consumed.

Things didn't always turn out so well for the cat and their owners. In 1896 Phoenix, Arizona Territory, young Juan Encinas thought it might be fun to throw the family tabby into a well. Grabbing the feline's tail, he leaned over the well, but lost his balance, falling in with the flailing cat in his hand. His fall and his leg were broken by the splash into three feet of water. According to the newspaper reports, "the cat made matters unpleasant by jumping on his head to keep out of the water and badly scratching him." Boy and cat remained in the well for an hour until they were discovered and rescued. Reported the *Arizona*

Republic, "A rope was lowered, and he was hauled to the surface along with his four-legged companion in misery. The boy's face was a sight—deep furrows showing how kitty took revenge for the impromptu bath. The lad's leg is in a condition to keep him out of mischief for several weeks."

At least that cat survived, but not so the kitty of the two little daughters of La Grande, Oregon, City Councilman William Getchell. The girls moved their play from the parlor into the kitchen, not knowing the house cat had crawled in the oven of the wood cook stove. The sisters closed the oven door and started a fire. A half hour later, the smell of burning hair alerted folks something was wrong. "Upon investigation," the *La Grande Observer* reported, "the cat was found to be baked to a nice brown, and, though dead, was 'a very warm thing'."

Of all the cat stories in frontier newspapers—and there are millions of them per *Cat Tales of the Old West*—none is more amazing than that of little Annie McGinn of West Butte, Montana, and her unnamed kitten that she adorned with a ribbon and tiny bell around its neck. The girl and her furry friend were playing near a shaft adjacent to the big Poulin mine hoist one day when something startled the pussycat, which leaped from her caretaker into the hole. Annie raced to find her brother, who lowered a rope into the shaft, "hoping that the kitten would 'catch on' and be hoisted, but the cat only howled louder."

Unable to rescue her pet, Annie daily carried bits of meat and bread to the shaft, dropping them down for the kitty to eat, but after a couple weeks, the feline's whimpers and moans ceased, and Annie "gave up her pet as lost forever, and Christmas at Annie's home was not as cheerful for the owner of the lost kitten as it might have been had kitty not been so venturesome."

After the kitten's whimpers stopped at the shaft, miners over the coming months at the Green Mountain, Mountain Con, Anaconda, Mountain View, Gray Rock, Modoc, Mountain Chief, Rarus and other working mines periodically "heard sounds similar to those made by a sick infant."

Four months later "while some children were playing near the dump of the Colusa mine, they were startled upon beholding a cat tumbling down the pile of rocks with a cart load of waste that had just been dumped." As the *Anaconda Standard* reported, "The cat meowed piteously as it rolled over just in time to escape a big chunk that came bounding past." The children raced to the rescue and "found a sorry-looking species of the cat family" with matted and soiled hair, red eyes, and sore feet and legs. Its only identifying mark was a little ribbon with the attached brass bell tied to its neck. The kitten had wandered through the labyrinthine mine shafts for four months and had walked countless miles before seeing daylight more than two miles from the shaft where she had originally fallen. Kitten and Annie were reunited with the ecstatic joy of both.

Back then, as today, a spirited debate raged over the relative merits of cats versus dogs. In 1887 Great Falls, Montana, a young boy who kept "cats of several colors and sizes" decided he needed a change as he stroked one of his felines in his lap. "Mamma," he announced, "I hope the next cat I have will be a dog!"

In 1889 Salem, Oregon, one young boy felt compelled to write the *Capital Journal* an essay on the value of dogs versus cats. Wrote the pintsized observer, "I'd rather have a dog than a cat any day. Dogs can race cats; they can race other dogs; they can race boys or anything. Nobody ain't scared of a cat. A mouse is, but not if it ain't somewheres that it can't get out of, or a rat either. A dog can make a cat dead if he bites her enough. When he comes in the yard, he can make her tail look like a Christmas tree. He can make her fix her back up like a camel. I ain't afraid of thieves, but thieves are afraid of dogs. If a thief comes where a dog can get at him, he'll run; but the dog won't run. A dog can watch a house better than a policeman. He won't let the dog that owns it come in the back yard in the middle of the night; but a cat would. If a man or any other thief was to sneak in, would a cat care? She'd go over the fence like lightning. That's what. A dog knows when you're home from school. He ain't sleepy then. He has fun with old hats, if you give him one. You've got to pay for keeping him, but you don't a cat, because a dog's some good and a cat ain't. I'd rather have a dog."

Despite the boy's eloquence, not everyone trusted dogs over cats. In 1896 San Francisco, a local woman spotted a big black dog jumping toward a six-year-old boy, who screamed and stood petrified from fear the canine would attack. Realizing the lad's danger, the woman picked up a round stone and tossed it at the canine. Though she missed the dog, he spun around and raced away as fast as he could until he reached the rock. Picking it up with his teeth, the mongrel trotted back to the woman and laid it at her feet, wagging his tail for the woman to throw it again. It seems all the dog wanted to do was play fetch with the little boy.

Chapter Three

Fun and Danger

Throughout the ages, children have loved to play
games as a source of fun, laughter, and education,
though they seldom recognized it as such for the
latter. Pintsized pioneers were no different. They laughed,
they learned, and they entertained themselves whenever
they had spare time, mostly with their siblings or, when
they could, with their neighbors and schoolmates. Sure,
they had many chores to do, but play remained the primary
job of any frontier youngster. Recreation helped kids make
decisions and think critically as their little minds and
brains developed. Play taught social skills like empathy,
compromise, teamwork, and conflict resolution as their
personalities developed. Physically, recreation developed
coordination, strength, and stamina, all traits they would
need as adults to adapt to a challenging and tough
environment. Whether playing jacks or winning at
marbles, little kids learned persistence, focus, and the joy
of achievement, lessons that would help them later in life
as productive adults.

The little pioneers, like their counterparts east of the
Mississippi River, played games that were sometimes
centuries old like jacks, marbles, leap frog, hide and seek,

jump rope, and others. Not realizing the consequences of their activities, they improvised "imitation games" by replicating slices of frontier life based on what they saw at home or what they observed in their communities. Some of the imitation games they played—as documented by period newspapers—included horse thieves, wild west shows, lynching, and hog-killings, sometimes with fatal results. Frontier games for children had their many pleasures, but they also carried tragic hazards that provided sobering lessons and, sometimes, emotional trauma that plagued the youngsters well into their adult lives. Often their recreation could be described as homemade frontier fun and danger.

Among the various outdoor games appealing to frontier children, "crack the whip" was one of the most popular in the schoolyard, on the street, or around the pasture, as it required no equipment and offered both thrills and spills. Though both boys and girls played it, males favored the game because of its rough-and-tumble energy. Children started the game by grabbing hands or linking arms, then forming a single line, usually with the biggest and strongest child at the head of the string. Then the leader ran in circular or zigzag patterns. As the speed increased, the centrifugal force intensified until it "cracked the whip" and flung trailing participants out of the adolescent train. The kids tumbled across the playground with mirthful exuberance. Besides laughter, the exercise also generated broken bones, chipped teeth, cracked kneecaps, bruises, grass burns, and even torn clothes for mother to mend.

The 1889 *Advertiser* in Sturgis, Dakota Territory, noted, "There are very few children belonging to the public schools in country districts, and very few men and women who have, in their day, belonged to them who have not had the 'fun' of being switched off the end of a long line of boys and girls while playing 'crack the whip.' It is a well-grounded belief that more stars have been seen by this process than were ever viewed through all of the great telescopes combined, and not a few children have taken their last hurried view of earth and sky while flying round on the tail of the animal 'whip,' with steps out of all proportion to the length of their legs. However, most of the participants have survived the sport through the providence that watches over fools and children."

In the 1890s alone, hundreds of pioneer children—or "crackers" as the players were sometimes called—fell casualty to participation across the West. In Brenham, Texas, Clare Taylor broke his left arm near the wrist on his school grounds. Kansas casualties included John Becker in White City with a dislocated wrist; Vernie Morely of Clyde with a fractured collarbone; and Myrtie Bellows of Grenola with a concussion and head injury. Kansan Clarence Shaw "was thrown against a tree and received injuries so severe that a physician was called." Poor little Tot Chatham broke her collarbone playing the game in Osage City, Kansas, then re-broke it a few days later "while attempting to ride a wheel," according to newspaper accounts.

Crack-the-whip injuries accrued throughout the 1890s West. Robbie Nathan broke his arm playing the game in Great Falls, Montana. William Anderson "was cracked against the washboard, breaking his nose. Dr. Davis mended the cracker" in Albany, Oregon. Boise, Idaho, schoolboy Sol Turley "was thrown against a passing vehicle, breaking the bridge of his nose." Nine-year-old Elwood Beebe of Provo, Utah, "was thrown violently to the ground and sustained a very bad fracture of the collar bone." On a Randolph, Nebraska, schoolyard, "a little girl was thrown and hurt so badly that she remained unconscious for several hours. The physicians think there is no possible hope for her recovery." In Newcastle,

Wyoming, Harry Camplin sustained head injuries after "being thrown on the hillside while playing crack the whip at school." Linwood Durrett of Slater, Missouri, broke his leg between the knee and the ankle while involved in the amusement.

The game was dangerous enough when played on playgrounds and in pastures, but even more so when performed on city streets. The *Anaconda Standard* six days before Christmas of 1898 described one such incident: "A dozen small boys were playing 'crack the whip' last night in front of the opera house. They would form a chain by holding onto each other's coattails. The leader would dart out into the middle of the street, turn suddenly to one side and dart back again towards the sidewalk, and the smallest boy at the tail-end would be hurled around at a rapid rate. The process was repeated several times, and the little boys laughed. Once the crack of the whip came near to resulting disastrously. By the jerk of the chain, the four who formed the 'snapper' parted from the others, and away they rolled out into the street just in front of a street car that was speeding westward. The motorman applied the brakes just in time, for no sooner had the little snappers cleared the rails than the car passed the point where a moment before it looked like the day before a funeral."

Youngsters also played the game during the winter, either on frozen ponds or ice-skating rinks. Young H. Mason nursed a broken leg after "playing crack the whip on the skating rink last Sunday" in Salt Lake City. Noted the *Salt Lake Herald*, "This crack-the-whip game has been quite popular among the skaters this winter, but we are inclined to think that this accident may cause it to become unpopular to a certain extent at least." In Deadwood, South Dakota, ten-year-old Harry Gantz was cracked into the railing in a local skating rink and "received a cut of about an inch in length directly over the right eye."

A less dangerous game, "Annie over," sometimes referenced as "auntie over," "ante over," or "andy over," was a high-flying game of tag, requiring a simple ball and some type of obstacle such as a free-standing house, a barn, a school house, or even a Conestoga wagon on the route west. Participants split into two teams and started out on opposite sides of the house or structure. The team with the ball, which could be of rubber, a sock or even an inflated pig's bladder, yelled "annie" and the other team responded "over." The team with the ball threw it over the structure or wagon. If no one caught the ball on the other side, the process repeated. If a player caught the ball, he and his teammates ran around the obstacle and tried to tag their opponents with the ball. Once tagged, an opponent was either out or switched allegiance to the other team. The game continued until all the players were eliminated on one team.

Another common outdoor activity was "goose and gander" where a "mother goose" was selected to protect the other children or "her goslings" from the "gander." The goslings would line up behind their mother goose and hold the waist or shoulders of the person in front of them. Then the gander would charge the line, trying to touch or grab goslings while their protector shielded them from the attacker. The game ended when all the goslings had been captured.

"Leap frog" was another fun game that provided exercise and could be played with as few as two children, usually boys. Participants would squat and lean forward on their hands, resembling a frog on a lily pad. Another player would spread his legs and hop over them, placing his hands briefly on the back of the crouched child for balance. Once a player had cleared all the participants in the frog line, he would then assume the crouching position for other players to leap over him. The object of the game varied, sometimes to see how far the group could move before someone tripped or how long they could go without having to take a breather.

The physical nature of leap frog appealed more to boys. Further, it was considered in many areas of the West to be "unladylike" for girls in skirts to take part in the potentially immodest activity. By the mid-1890s, when bloomers had become accepted female attire, the *San Diego Sun* reported on a supposed conversation between a gentleman conversing with a young lady after surveying her new bloomers. "I suppose you are happy now," he observed. When she asked him to explain, he replied, "You must have the freedom of movement for which you have longed all your life.... Ever since you were a little girl, you say, you have had a longing to play leap frog and all such games every time you saw the boys doing it ... And you always thought it unjust that you should be deprived of such sport because you were a girl."

She replied, "I admit it. It did seem so."

"Well, now you have got your bloomers, I suppose there is no reason why you shouldn't play leap frog if you want to. Why don't you do it?"

"Because now that I can, I don't see any fun in it," she replied.

While leap frog may have been the domain of boys, jump rope and hopscotch appealed more to young girls. Both were physical like leap frog, but girls developed chants or rhymes as they played, increasing the rhythm, though not always the harmony among the participants.

A girl with a store-bought jump rope, a length of lariat or, even better, a section of her mother's clothes line could play the game. Though it could be played individually, it was more fun with greater options when multiple young ladies participated, and the tasks were divided between jumpers and turners, the ones who twirled the rope.

One of the more popular variations of the game was called "pepper, salt, mustard, cider, vinegar." First two players are chosen by lot to twirl the rope. The other girls jump by turns, saying, with increasing rapidity, "pepper, salt, mustard, cider, vinegar" as the rope spins faster and faster until the jumper trips up.

Another version was "huckery buck," or "huck a buck." Again, two participants twirled the rope while others jump in and out as quickly as they can until they make a misstep. One or multiple jumpers could play "skip the ladder" where the players lands first on one foot and next on the other.

In "rock the cradle" the rope swings in a pendulum motion and the girl jumps in and out of the cord's path. "Going a visiting" begins with one girl spinning the rope over herself when a second lass hops in and jumps with her before leaping back out. In "change bedrooms" two girls turn the rope and two others jump in. The two jumpers must swap places while rope revolves, a difficult feat.

Another variation is "going to school" where two girls lock arms or hold hands and, with their free hands twirl the rope, taking a variety of fast and slow steps as they jump. "Bake the bread" offers a variation where the jumper enters the twirling pattern with a stone or a stick, which she drops and then picks up without tripping over the rope.

A summary of jump rope games in an 1888 fall edition of the *Houston Post* described how girls much preferred to be the jumper rather than the twirler, creating some ethical challenges for the players. "Where several girls are playing, the one who trips must take her turn at the rope," the *Post* reported. "This is a great test of a girl's temper. If she doesn't 'play fair,' she will deny it when she trips. Then the other girls get mad, and they won't play, or they put her out of the game for cheating. Then she learns the value of truth. If she is not caught in lying, however, she is very apt to try it again, and may in time become adept at sly lying. But the chances are that the other little girls will find her out if she does not fib with great skill and discernment. Truly, it is a very great temptation to a little girl to tell stories under such circumstances, but like all other temptations, it is one that a good little girl will learn to resist. She will take her end of rope with resignation when her turn comes."

The *Post* article also raised the question of karma related to the source of the young lass's jump rope. "Most little girls can persuade parents or relatives to purchase for them at the toy stores nice jumping ropes with neatly trimmed wooden handles. But, when such ropes are not to be had, bad little girls have been known to steal parts of their mothers' clotheslines. When a little girl who has cut a clothesline falls and gets hurt, she is apt to be looked upon as the victim of a special providence. Yet it must be admitted that many good girls, who are not skillful, often fall, so that the final cause of tripping is still a bone of contention among both philosophers and theologians."

A year earlier, in the same newspaper, an observer from an earlier generation noted how skillful girl jumpers had gotten, being able to manage the challenge of the jumping ropes while wearing roller skates. "Just look at them girls jumping rope with wheels tied to their shoes, and, by hokey, they jump two ropes going different ways at the same time. When I was a lad, it was as much as we could do to jump one rope with our plain shoes on."

By the 1880s, jump rope was so intense among girls that some health professionals worried about the dangers of sustained jumping. One western surgeon was concerned that the activity "produces a continuous concussion of the joints in the spinal column of a dangerous character, often resulting in inflammation and necrosis of the bone, deformity, and death." He concluded, "I would warn children against rope dancing, and advise parents to prohibit it under all circumstances." Other experts recommended jumping in moderation, not hundreds of times in a row until they fall from exhaustion, noting that "the jar and jolt of the internal organs is a terrible strain, even on the strongest system."

Hopscotch was less intense than jump rope and equally suited for young boys and girls, but the lasses gravitated to it more than the lads. Again, part of the appeal was that girls often cited chants or rhymes as they played. Hopscotch required players to scratch out nine staggered blocks—two in the first row, one in the second, two in the third row, one in the fourth, two in the fifth and one in the sixth—in the ground. Players took turns tossing the marker into each numbered square, then hopping into each row—except the one with the marker in it—on one or two feet. When they reached the last square, they spun around and hopped back, again missing the marked square but stopping by it to pick up the marker and hop back to the starting line. If they stepped on a line, lost their balance or missed the mark, they lost their turn. It was a simple game, but it helped teach balance and coordination.

Pioneer girls relished certain games, and pioneer boys preferred others. Girls enjoyed such pastimes as jackstones and jackstraws, known to later generations as jacks and pick-up sticks, respectively, while boys liked marbles and mumblety-peg, also known as mumble peg or mumble-the-peg.

Frontier jacks were played with pieces like dried beans, small stones, carved pieces of wood or small bones and a walnut-sized ball made of whatever was handy, including leather, yarn, cloth, and even rubber when available from local merchants. Using five to ten of the so-called jackstones, a girl would toss them on the ground. The object was to pick up a specific number of bones in sequence after tossing the ball in the air and then catch the ball with the same hand before it hit the ground. When afforded a ball that actually bounced off the floor, girls might opt to catch the ball after the first bounce. In the first round, the girl would pick up the jacks one at a time, then two at a time and three at a time until she ran through all of the bones or missed the ball. The winner was the girl who finished the highest number of sets without making a mistake.

Girls played jacks all the time, certainly not a newsworthy item unless the young ones swallowed one of the pieces, which happened more frequently than you might imagine. For instance, after a three-year-old girl in her country home outside Hanford, California, swallowed a jackstone, "her father took her quickly to the nearest doctor. The country doctor instantly stood the child upon her head. She was seized with a fit of coughing, when out flew the jackstone, and the child's life was saved." In another California incident outside Sacramento, a young girl named Mereed Dulard swallowed a store-bought jackstone with six prongs. Reported the *Pacific Bee*, "It stuck fast in her throat, and for a while the girl was in danger of choking to death, but a full emetic saved her life" by forcing her to vomit and dislodge the play piece.

The *Blade* of Chanute, Kansas, wryly pointed out the problem in a piece titled "Foreign Bodies in Throat." Wrote the *Blade*, "Children, who act on the belief that the mouth was made before pockets, often make it a receptacle for objects of all shapes, sizes, and conditions of cleanliness—pins, jackstones, marbles, coins, and other things innumerable. Usually such treasures are found when wanted, but sometimes they act as in other pockets with a hole in the bottom—they drop out, or rather they drop in, and then trouble ensues."

Less troublesome for girls were "jackstraws" or what we would today call "pick-up sticks." The object was to drop them on the ground or floor, then retrieve them one at a time without moving another stick during the withdrawal. Whoever retrieved the most sticks without disturbing the others won the round. The game could be played indoors or out and was a favorite female pastime during frigid winter evenings on the frontier. As the game required patience and precision, it appealed more to girls than rowdy boys.

By contrast, boys gravitated to various games of marbles, which involved more action and elements of the frontier gambling culture, if played "for keeps." The most common game of marbles was "ringer," where the players marked off a circle three to ten feet in diameter in the ground or on the floor. Each player placed a specified number—often thirteen—of his marbles in the ring. Then, with a larger marble called a "shooter" or a "taw," each player tried to knock out of the ring as many of his opponents' marbles as possible. As long as a player knocked marbles out of the ring, he kept shooting. Whoever "captured" the most marbles from the circle was crowned the winner. Many games were played "for keeps" so that players retained any marbles they knocked from the ring, a form of juvenile gambling.

The *Pioneer-Times* of Deadwood, Dakota Territory, reported in July 1877, "Gambling seems to be a prevailing weakness of mankind. It seems to permeate humanity from boyhood up. While our men are busily engaged in 'bucking' against the capricious fortune of faro, our small boys are staking their worldly all on marbles. In fancy, we see Cain and Abel as small boys playing for 'keeps' in the garden of Eden."

Frontier boys carried their marbles in leather or cloth pouches and developed a variety of nicknames for the little orbs, depending on the composition. Clay marbles were called "commonies" or "mudballs," and wooden ones were known as "woodies." Stone marbles became "stoneys" or "chinas," while agate marbles made from banded agate or chalcedony stone carried the name of "flints." Glass marbles were known as "clearies," "swirls," or "glasses," while steel marbles were called "steelies." Small marbles were labeled as "peewees."

"Marbles, marbles everywhere," reported South Dakota's *Miller Press* in early March 1895. "On the street corners, in the alleys, and in the door yards, boys are playing the game of marbles handed down from one generation to another." In many communities, the emergence of lads shooting marbles was as sure a sign of spring's arrival as the appearance of wild flowers. South Dakota's *Lead Daily Call* a month earlier had observed, "The first approach of spring here is to see the young boys playing marbles. Every day, the street corners and sidewalks are thronged with the small boy and his festive marble. Even a dry spot two feet in diameter in the street is taken advantage of. This is a sure sign of spring, the groundhog to the contrary notwithstanding." A March issue of the Chanute, Kansas, *Daily Tribune* observed, "Spring is coming! Had you noticed it? We saw the heralds yesterday in a number of small boys playing marbles bare-headed and with bare feet." According to an 1891 report in the *Union County Courier* of Elk Point, South Dakota, "Spring has come in earnest; the boys are playing marbles."

Young boys' marble activities even reflected the technological advancements of the day as the *Black Hills Weekly Journal* in Dakota Territory noted in a February 1887 blurb: "The novel sight of boys playing marbles by electric light was witnessed at the corner of St. Joe and Sixth streets last night."

Noting the report of an Ohio school board prohibiting girls from skipping rope because of claims it damaged their health, the *Weekly Pioneer* in Deadwood, observed, "Better put the ki-bosh on the boys playing marbles—it wears out their thumb nails."

Not everyone thought marbles was an innocent game. The pastime was a problem for at least one 1895 Missouri legislator who introduced a bill prohibiting boys from playing marbles on Sunday. Commented the *Blackwell Daily Times-Record* in neighboring Oklahoma, "The Missouri legislation is running the morality business into the ground." Nor did all parents agree the game was harmless. The *Austin American-Statesman* in June 1881 noted, "Two small boys playing marbles in the alley leading down from the jail yesterday morning came to grief and retired from the field of action, looking as dismal as possible. The father of one of the boys created the trouble." Some even questioned when the game was played, like the *Bee* of Frankfort, Kansas, reporting in March 1887 that "at three o'clock Thursday morning of last week, when the moon was shining clear and bright, we espied half a dozen boys playing marbles in Mr. Frybarger's back yard." In 1893 Albuquerque, New Mexico Territory, during recess at the Fourth Ward public school, a dispute over a marbles game led to a stabbing when Leo Gibson pulled his pocketknife and gouged Leo Armijo in the neck. Armijo survived after doctors tended him and closed the wound with more than fifteen stitches. His attacker escaped town on a stolen horse.

As pocketknives were common and prized possessions among frontier boys, mumblety-peg allowed boys to develop their skills and their hand-eye coordination with a knife. In its simplest state, a boy would spin a knife to stick in the ground. If he succeeded and his opponent didn't, the loser had to stoop and pull the knife or a substitute peg from the ground with his teeth, hence the name and variations "mumble peg" and "mumble-the-peg." In other versions of the game, the boys drove a peg into the ground and whoever failed to duplicate a knife-throwing trick had to extract the peg with his teeth. It was an odd game, unsanitary and potentially embarrassing to the boys, especially when girls were around to watch them mumble the peg and pull it from the ground. It could also be dangerous as two boys playing mumblety-peg found out when one of them tripped and fell on his knife, inflicting a serious wound in his chest.

A June 1891 article in the Lawrence, Kansas, *Journal* advocated the use of child labor to offset the shortage of strawberry pickers that season. "There are, at this time in the year, many unemployed men and women, as a rule, and now that the schools are out, there are hundreds of boys and girls who could earn quite a little sum in this pleasant work. Pleasant work is used advisedly, the work being not at all laborious, and requiring scarcely no training except to remove the decayed berries from the vines and practice care in handling the plants. To a youngster, the work is not even tiresome, as stooping over is an easy posture, besides, they may get down on their knees as they are wont in playing mumblety-peg, or playing marbles or making mud pies."

As early as April 1875, the *Independent* of Helena, Montana, listed the "seasonable signs" of spring as "the moral mumble peg; the scientific play of marbles; and the vigorous game of hopscotch, have appeared upon the native heath."

With improving weather, pioneer boys and girls could also turn to the skies for hours of entertainment with kites. "It is a pleasant sensation to sit in the first spring sunshine and feel the steady pull of a good kite upon the string, and watch its graceful movements as it sways from side to side, ever mounting higher and higher, as if impatient to free itself and soar away amid the clouds," wrote Daniel Carter Beard in the chapter on kites in his *American Boy's Handy Book*. The only thing better than flying a kite, he believed, was sending a homemade one aloft. Beard's 1882 book provided instructions for kids to make kites shaped like men, women, children, frogs, butterflies, fish, king crabs, turtles, and Chinese dragons. He also offered guidelines for kites in various geometric shapes, including shields, stars, squares, and triangles. Beard even gave instructions on building "war" kites to attack and destroy other kites, an idea a Galveston paper claimed as originating in Texas.

Proclaimed the *Galveston Daily News*, "Kite-flying in Texas is accompanied by a new wrinkle which has not yet been acquired by the ambitious youth of more northern climes. In Texas, the tail of the kite is adorned with sundry glittering cutters or pieces of glass, which are very useful in severing the string of some other kite belonging to some other boy. This peculiarity is borrowed from the Mexicans. The idea is that there can be no real fun unless it creates disappointment or pain in the breast of some fellow being. As soon as a boy has got his kite well up in the air, some other boy feels it a duty he owes the country to allow his kite gracefully to descend until its tail can be brought to bear on the sting of the first kite. The knives or cutters sever the string and the boy loses his kite, much to the joy of the party of the second part. This new feature invests kite-flying with such an absorbing interest that it is almost impossible to keep a boy in the house during the preponderance of the kite epidemic. It has been suggested that there is only one really effective way of keeping the average boy from flying kites, and that is by extending him on a hard surface and placing railroad iron to the height of twenty feet upon his prostrate body. The principal objection is the expense of procuring the iron, which places the remedy beyond the reach of all but the wealthy."

Kites were so popular that by 1896 the national weather bureau, which used kites in its weather research and forecasting, was issuing "an illustrated pamphlet, describing how to make its high-flying kites for the benefit of the boys of the country."

Galveston *Daily News* in March 1881 observed, "Just now the American youth, and more particularly the Galveston boy, spends all of his leisure hours in flying kites. In this country, kite-flying is a favorite amusement of the rising generation. When the telegraph lines are festooned with garlands composed of the tails of wrecked kites; when the wheels of runaway turnouts are frescoed with the brains of unwary pedestrians; the cause being horses taking fright from kites; when everything in the house is daubed all over with paste, and the boy goes about with bloodshot eyes from gazing at the bright orb of day that hangs resplendent in the blue vault above, the kite time has come."

In 1888 C.B. Shilling reminisced for *The Arrow* of Wichita, Kansas, about his fondness for kite-flying as a boy. "You may talk as you please of the pleasures of childhood, from spinning a top to playing leap frog, from going nest hunting in the deep tangled wild-wood, and poking the bees from under a log. But of all the old sports which I still can remember, amidst growing cares and years in their flight, is when with the boys on a day in September, so gloriously happy I got out my kite." By November of 1894, the *El Paso Times* defended grown men for flying kites for the health benefits. "Do not be astonished," reported the paper, "at old men flying kites, spinning tops or indulging in other childish games. It is not only a custom of the land, but it is recommended by the sages and doctors of the country as an aid to heal and a preservative of youth."

Children, though, were not always as careful or as lucky as their older counterparts and sustained multiple injuries, especially in cities with proliferating telegraph and electric wires. In Galveston, Texas, ten-year-old Mattie Falby was badly burned by an electric wire while flying a kite. His kite string became entangled in the telegraph wire, which touched the electric wire as he tried to free his kite. The shock severely burned both hands. The attending physician feared amputation might be necessary to save the lad's life. Less serious was an Austin accident where one boy was flying his kite when a sudden gust of wind sent it into a dive that struck another boy, knocking him down and leaving an ugly gash on the top of his head. In 1885 San Antonio, a little boy named Frank Krueger fell off a roof while flying a kite and injured himself seriously, according to newspaper reports. In St. Louis, twelve-year-old Louisa Schwartz was flying a kite near a deep catchment basin for water. While trying to steer her kite, she backed off the ledge into the pool of water and did not surface again. Her body was recovered two hours later. While flying a kite during a heavy electrical storm near Kansas City, Kansas, twelve-year-old Walter Vinson was struck by lightning and killed instantly.

The *Arizona Weekly Citizen* in 1893 described the aftermath of one kiting incident: "Little Earle Wilkinson has his arm in a sling. He is not carrying it that way for fun, but on account of an accident he met with. He was flying a kite from the roof of a house and fell off before he knew where he was. His wounds are not dangerous."

Not only did children flying kites harm themselves, they injured and killed adults as well, most commonly, from spooking horses and teams. Observed the *San Antonio Light* in February 1885, "The season of flying kites is upon us, and several runaway teams will probably be the consequence." Indeed they were. In Hartford, Kansas, a flying kite dropped onto a team of horses pulling a buggy. The terrified horses overturned the buggy, spilling the occupants onto the ground. According to the newspaper account, "The horses then ran away, smashing the buggy and hurting themselves so that they are valueless. Flying kites in town is not without danger."

In Ottawa, Kansas, an 1896 *Herald* newspaper headline read, "A Horse Frightened by a Flying Kite Causes Disaster." An area woman and her visiting brother were injured in a series of events instigated "by a flying kite in the hands of some frolicsome boys." The horse became terrified and unmanageable "by the sudden darting of a kite across the road" and bolted away. Running wild, the animal wrecked the buggy and dumped the occupants, leaving the woman with three broken ribs and her brother with a bruised shoulder and strained neck.

A runaway accident in Sacramento, California, in 1868, took the life of a 56-year-old Patrick Ham when his spooked horse tossed him from his wagon, which then ran over the man and produced injuries that proved fatal within two hours. Five or six boys were seen flying kites at the intersection where the horse bolted away. As they disappeared immediately after the accident, the boys were believed to be responsible for the fatality.

Despite the troublesome problems with kite-flying, the *Daily Traveler* of Arkansas City, Kansas, offered observations and an 1896 spring plea for boys and their kites. Wrote the newspaper, "Kite-flying time has rolled around once again and the boys all over the city are making the most of it, putting in their spare hours sailing kites. Kansas is especially adapted to flying kites successfully. The Kansas zephyrs, which gambol over our broad, fertile prairies, will make anything go up—except the price of real estate—if you only tie a string onto it and hold on. Kite-flying time is very dear to the average youngsters, and how soon it rolls around. Many boys, who are flying their kites high this season, will be too big to indulge in the sport next year. Many of them will be called to commence the struggle for existence. At its best, there are only a few kite-flying seasons in a boy's life. Let him enjoy it while he can."

One of the most unusual kite stories appeared in an 1887 summer edition of the *Abilene Reporter* in Texas and variations of the story appeared across the country under headlines such as "A Latter Day Miracle" in the *Brooklyn Citizen*, "A Texas Yarn" in the *Cleveland Plain-Dealer*, "Benjamin Franklin Discounted" in the *San Francisco Examiner* and "A Hard Story to Swallow" in the *Chicago Herald*. The story even made it across the Atlantic, appearing in the *Evening Express* in Liverpool, England.

The *Abilene Reporter* story, published amid a Texas drought, read: "Two boys were flying kites. One of the lads, named Yessup, when about four hundred yards of string had been paid out, asked his father to write a message and send it up to the kite. The old man sat down and wrote this: 'Send some rain. Yessup.' The message climbed up the string. A bird circling high in the air winged its way to the bit of paper, which it pecked viciously. An hour later, the kite was hauled in by the boy. The paper was in tatters, the only part of the message remaining intact being this portion of the signature: 'Yes.' Two hours later, a southeaster came up, and the rain fell in torrents."

Kite-flying like many other established recreations and games was seasonal, an observation made as early as 1868 by the *Sacramento Bee*, which reported, "Boys fly kites and trundle hoops in early spring; hopscotch and marbles follow later in the season. Then comes baseball, and after it mumblety-peg and jackstones." However, frontier children made up games from what they had seen and experienced on the frontier. These "imitation" games were often humorous, but sometimes as deadly as the events, which spawned them.

Charles A. Siringo grew up on the Matagorda Bay in Texas and imitated the cowboys he had seen in the area while going to school. To get to school, he would take a route by the beach. "I would generally be late at school, for there were so many little thing to detain me ... while I was riding along on my stick horse taking the kinks out of my rope, a piece of fish line, so as to be ready to take in the first crab that showed himself. Those crabs went in large droves and sometimes venture quite a distance out from the Gulf, but on seeing a person would break for the water. It was not long before I spied a large drove on ahead, pulling their freight for the water. I put spurs to my pony and dashed after them. I managed to get one old fat fellow headed off and turned toward the prairie. I threw at him several times, but he would always go through the loop before I could pull it up. He finally struck a hole and disappeared."

Continued Siringo, "I was determined to get him out and take another whirl at him, so dropping my horse and getting on all fours, I began digging the sand away with my hands, dog fashion ... Every now and then, I would play dog by sticking my snoot down in the hole to smell. But I rammed it down once too often. Mr. Crab was nearer the surface than I thought, for he was laying for me. I gave a Comanche yell, jumped ten feet in the air and lit out for home at a two-forty gait. One of his claws was fastened to my upper lip while the other clamped my nose with an iron-like grip."

A passing neighbor saw Siringo's predicament and broke the crab legs to free young Charlie from its grip. To make matters worse, Siringo received a spanking from his teacher for being late. As he described the punishment, "He laid me across his knee and made me think a nest of bumble bees were having a dance on the seat of my breeches."

Sometimes, imitation play affected parents like the story reported in an 1886 Texas newspaper of a saloon keeper returning home to find his wife away running errands and his three sons all under the age of nine playing "keep saloon" in the backyard beside a bench lined with bottles and a pail of liquid that turned out to be beer. The youngest son stood with a towel wrapped around his waist and was dipping beer from the pail for his brothers and neighbor playmates, who were tipsy or passed out.

"Boys, you must not drink that," he scolded, but his six-year-old "bartending" son replied, "We's playin' s'loon, papa, and I was selling it just like you." After returning all the neighbor boys home and seeing his own sons to bed, the saloonkeeper wept until his wife returned. After explaining what had happened in her absence, the saloon owner returned to town and sold out his business. Back home, he vowed never to sell or drink another drop of liquor so he would be a better example for his three sons.

In 1888, the *Arkansas Traveler* reported a similar incident where a father returned home half-intoxicated to find his son and daughter playing in their yard. "Now you be ma," said the boy, "and I'll be pa. Now you sit here, and I'll come home drunk."

The boy slipped away and returned, staggering with a water-filled bottle. Said the little girl to her father-imitating brother, "You promised ... that you wouldn't drink any more. The children are almost ragged, but you still throw your money away. Don't you know you are breaking my heart?"

Embarrassed by their lifelike imitation of him and his wife, the father "could think of nothing all day" but what he had overheard from his son's and daughter's play. After that, the touched father said, "I vowed I would not take another drink, and I will not."

However, many stories of imitation play had a tragic ending, especially when guns were involved. But guns were so commonplace as to almost be overlooked, but they turned up daily. Harvey Fergusson, who grew up in New Mexico Territory in the 1890s, and became a Western writer, remembered, "Nearly all boys then played with weapons more or less, and most of the older boys owned guns." But just because they may have played with guns and owned some didn't mean the boys—or the girls—always used them safely.

An unfortunate number of deaths resulted from siblings playing with guns. In Valentine, Texas, the older son of J.M. Tally while playing with a rifle shot and killed his two-year-old brother. Near Rush in Oklahoma Territory, ten-year-old Johnnie Clark slayed his fifteen-year-old brother Samuel Clark after pulling the trigger on a gun he thought was unloaded. In Oregon, Mrs. Emma McCoy was shot and killed by her fifteen-year-old daughter, who was playing with a rifle when it fired, the bullet piercing the mother's brain.

Outside of Dawson, Missouri, ten-year-old Joseph Fullenwider found a rusty revolver in a hay mow, picked it up and accidentally fired it, killing his brother John, five years old. Near Ophir, Utah, two little boys playing in an outhouse discovered a pistol. One of them picked it up and snapped the trigger at his five-year-old playmate named Duke, who later expired from the head wound. In San Jose, California, five-year-old Rebecca Smith and her ten-year-old brother were playing in the garret of their home when they discovered a revolver. The boy picked it up, pointed it at his sister and pulled the trigger with the usual results.

Accidental shootings were so common that newspapers ran headlines proclaiming "The Usual Result," "Same Old Story," "The Fatal 'Empty' Gun," "The Old Story Repeated," "Pathetic Tragedy," "It Was Loaded of Course," "It Went Off," "Killed His Brother," and "Accidentally Shot," perhaps the most common headline. Fatalities from accidental gunplay were so common that in 1880, the *Trinidad News* in Colorado published a concise adage on the danger:

> *Two little boys playing with a gun,*
> *The gun went off and then there was one*

Tragic as those deaths were, even more heart-rending were the fatalities that came from the "imitation" games the children often played. For instance, in the Black Hills near Rapid City in 1893, a pair of boys twelve and nine years old decided to play hunter. One of them picked up a fifty-caliber Spencer carbine that was standing between the cupboard and the wall in their dugout. Allie Boutwell cocked the hammer, pointed the gun at the younger Emory Stucker and pulled the trigger. The bullet from the supposedly unloaded carbine struck his young playmate between the mouth and the nose, killing him instantly. The death was ruled accidental, but it was typical of children's death and injury when loaded guns were around.

In West Plains, Missouri, two Hall brothers were playing hog-killing, which they had witnessed the day before. Playing the hog, one got on his hands and knees. The other put a pistol to his head and fired. The little fellow lived but a short time. In McMinnville, Oregon, the Smith brothers, ages twelve and five, decided to play "horse-thief." The elder brother pointed a shotgun at his younger brother and pulled the trigger, with tragic results. At Independence, Oregon, Dewitt McDuffie, twelve, shot eight-year-old Leopold Paulus with a shotgun while playing "robber." While pretending to be a "highwayman" near Kansas City, Floyd Nichols, fourteen, killed his thirteen-year-old cousin Charlie Wildermood with an "unloaded" revolver. In St. Joseph, Missouri, Claude Sheldon and Harry Stagg were imitating "Buffalo Bill." "This is the way Buffalo Bill does it," Stagg said while pointing the gun at his friend's head and pulling the trigger. The wound was not fatal, but tore one eye from its socket.

The western ethos, thanks to dime novels, was so pervasive that even boys back east died imitating frontier fantasies. In Detroit, Michigan, eleven-year-old Eddie Lapier died after being shot by Frank Lane, sixteen, while they and other boys played "Wild West." Another shooting occurred in Warren, Ohio, from boys playing "Jesse James." Harry Koehler was shot through the face, but survived, while his assailant, a boy named Richards in the title role of Jesse James, went to jail. In Thompsonville, Kentucky, boy's playing "Indian fighters" resulted in the deaths of Willie and Lee Haines, fourteen and twelve, respectively, at the hands of a playmate named Hamilton.

In 1893 Sioux Falls, South Dakota, two fourteen-year-old boys were playing "hanging." According to newspaper reports, "One was allowed to hang just a little too long and is now an angel."

The list of unfortunate frontier accidents goes on and on, demonstrating that while fun and games were a part of everyday life on the pintsized frontier, so was danger and death. Not every "imitation" game ended in tragedy, as was illustrated on a hot July day in 1874 Leavenworth, Kansas, when "a young chap named Augustus Dean" opted to play "Indian" and scare a group of neighborhood children playing in a front yard. Reported the

Leavenworth Times, "The little ones were almost frightened out of their wits, and their screams drew the attention of one of the parents, who took Augustus by the scalp, and dressed him down with a barrel stave, 'til he promised to leave forever the warpath, and remove his infernal toggery."

Chapter Four

Playing with Fire

As a five-year-old boy growing up on the Comstock Lode, John Taylor Waldorf remembered a town fire "was better than a circus," with its crackling and roaring flames. Looking back on his childhood years in his memoirs, he asked, "Did you ever run a mile to a fire and then feel keenly disappointed because the firemen had everything under control when you reached the scene?" or "Did you ever view a fire merely as a spectacle, without any thought of what it meant to the victims?" Then he answered his own question, stating, "If you never did, you were born grown up and had no childhood at all."

Looking back on his youthful adventures, Waldorf recalled the devastating Virginia City, Nevada, fire of October 26, 1875, which destroyed much of the mining town that was his home. In his recollections, he wrote, "My first fire was something to be remembered. I recall with regret the inability of the firemen to master it before it had desolated two-thirds of Virginia City, but I wasn't sorry the day it happened. I was five years old then, and the thought that hundreds of people were losing their homes never occurred to me. The fact that my own home didn't burn probably had much to do with the perfection of my enjoyment."

The abstract reasoning or conscience Waldorf developed as he matured into adulthood was absent as a youth, so he—like other children—didn't always comprehend, much less care about, the implications of a conflagration on the lives of other people or the potential dangers to themselves. Child play on the American frontier could quickly turn destructive or deadly, especially when youngsters failed to realize the consequences of their curiosity and their innocent activities. Such was the case in playing with fire, which on the frontier included explosives—such as gunpowder and dynamite—used in various pioneer occupations from road building to mining.

Pioneers utilized fireplaces, wood-burning stoves, lamps, lanterns, and candles to provide essential fire for cooking, heating, and illumination. The invention of friction matches in 1826 England and their introduction into the U.S. in the 1830s simplified fire-starting, making it child's play. Until then, it was a difficult procedure, using flint and steel to create a spark, which took to flame in tinder such as dried grass, wood shavings, or pieces of paper. As the tiny flame grew, it was nursed to life with kindling—small, thin strips of wood—and then fed larger pieces of firewood.

Matches—sometimes called "Lucifers" in their early iterations—made it so easy even a child could start a fire, and plenty did. By the middle of the nineteenth century, the safety match—which required a special striking surface to spark a flame—became available and affordable in the United States. By the 1870s and 1880s, matches could be purchased in general stores throughout the frontier and were commonplace in even remote homesteads. While safety matches may have been safer, they were not childproof. Accounts of fires started by "children playing with matches" pepper period newspapers.

In 1877 Bonham, Texas, youngsters experimenting with Lucifers in an upstairs room of the Charley Doss residence started a blaze that consumed the house. Noble efforts to save furniture and household items from the conflagration failed when the rescuers deposited the goods too near the dwelling, and they burned anyway. The residence carried a $2,500 valuation. Children playing with a lighted candle among some loose cotton in a backroom initiated a blaze that drove an elderly, bedridden man from his home in Moody, Texas, in 1885.

An 1888 fire in Suisun, California, destroyed $400,000 worth of property because of kids playing with matches in a barn. Careless children, again experimenting with Lucifers, in Sturgis, Dakota Territory, during the winter of 1888 started a fire in a Main Street restaurant. The conflagration spread to a nearby livery stable. The newspaper office, a tailor shop, and a Chinese laundry "were also wiped out in short order by the devouring flames," reported the *Custer Weekly Chronicle*. In 1893 Pueblo, Colorado, boys cavorting in the cupola atop the six-story Hotel Mesa under construction, created a blaze "which burned with tremendous speed" through alleged fireproof cement floors. The fire caused $100,000 in damage, five times the $20,000 insurance policy that partially covered the loss.

In 1891 Pittsburg, Kansas, children frolicking in the street set ablaze a pile of dry grass and paper near the boardwalk. "The fire caught the dry boards, making a lively blaze," the *Pittsburg Daily Headlight* reported before neighbors with buckets and tubs of water extinguished the flames and prevented their spread.

The spring of 1896 in Grand Junction, Colorado, boys playing in the neighborhood around Walter A. Abbey's residence one afternoon started a bonfire in a haystack behind the dwelling. A five o'clock alarm brought the fire department, and in minutes "a stream of water was soon playing on the stack and extinguished the flames."

In Portland, Oregon, Mrs. C.G. Carter in 1896 was alone with her seven-year-old daughter, who was cavorting around a lamp in their parlor. When she pulled the cloth from the table, the lamp fell on her and shattered at her feet, saturating her dress with oil and setting it on fire. Seizing an old blanket, her mother wrapped it around her daughter and quickly extinguished the flames. The girl escaped with a few burns on her hands, but was otherwise free of injury.

Three-year-old Bessie Gesner of Silverton, Oregon, set her dress on fire while experimenting with matches. The flames nearly burned her clothing off before they were doused. Though severely burned, Bessie survived, "the little sufferer ... getting along as well as could be expected," reported the *Salem Statesman Journal*.

The West's legendary towns weren't immune from juvenile firebugs, either. In May 1896, kids playing with matches destroyed a steam laundry in Deadwood, South Dakota. Tombstone may have been the town too tough to die, but it wasn't fireproof. Children toying with matches in an upstairs room of the *Tombstone Prospector* set fire to a stack of newspapers. The flames spread through the second floor and the first-floor ceiling before the volunteer fire department arrived and contained the damage to the building. Had the firemen arrived any later, reported the *Tombstone Epitaph*, "the place would have been a roaring furnace" and a threat to the entire community.

Town boys playing with matches under the wooden boardwalk in Mandan, North Dakota, in 1897 spawned a fire by Cooley's paint shop. The blaze spread and ultimately consumed three small hotels, a barbershop, and several small dwellings.

Some small boys fooling around near a Rapid City, Dakota Territory, corral tried to catch a mouse until it hid in a hole under some hay. One youngster had the bright idea of setting fire to the hay to drive the mouse out. The blaze whooshed through the hay, alerting nearby adults who turned in the fire alarm. The prompt action of the firemen saved the day by arriving quickly and extinguishing the fire. Reported the *Black Hills Weekly Journal*, "The ground was saved, the corral was damaged by being torn down, the little hay was burned, and the boys escaped. Nothing has been heard of the mouse." Damage totaled between five and ten dollars.

While young males may have started most of the child-spawned frontier fires, girls ignited several. A little girl playing with matches in Emporia, Kansas, burned down the barn of Frank O. Dowd of Sylvan Street in 1880. On the outskirts of Grants Pass, Oregon, a handful of girls playing with matches in an upstairs room of the George Burgess house set a tablecloth on fire, which spread to the rest of the house, destroying the structure and all its contents. A barn belonging to Knud Hanson of Logan Island, Utah, burned from a blaze started by girls playing with matches in 1882. In Wesson Springs, South Dakota, in the summer of 1891, another girl playing upstairs at the Wood home set fire to some carpet rags. The local newspaper reported the blaze was the "cause [of] no little excitement, but was noticed in time, and extinguished before very much damage was done."

Boys playing with matches in the Salt Lake City stable of pioneer Utah broom maker George Webster started a blaze that destroyed a thousand dollars' worth of broom hay, as well as fifty tons of fodder. Neighbors drove all the stock from the stable "except one pig, which was roasted," according to the *Salt Lake Herald*.

In 1890 Kansas, the *Sylvan Grove Sentinel* reported that children playing with matches in nearby Lincoln, Kansas, set ablaze a small barn near the train depot. "The loss was small, but the excitement for a few moments was great," the paper noted.

Not all losses from fires started by little or mischievous children were small, however. Sometimes the ensuing blazes destroyed entire neighborhoods and in some cases, even small towns. For instance, in 1898 Keeler, Nevada, an inferno caused by children playing with matches demolished two hotels and several adjoining houses. Reported the *Walker Lake Bulletin* in nearby Hawthorne, "This is a severe blow to Keller, as it is doubtful if the structures will be rebuilt."

Skidmore, a thriving village in Missouri's Nodaway County on July 23, 1885, "was almost totally destroyed by fire" that originated from "some boys playing in a hay mow and lighting some matches." Ninety minutes later, "the whole city was a mass of smoldering ruins," with twenty-three frame buildings demolished along with all their contents. Estimated losses totaled $70,000, equaling more than $2.3 million in 2025 dollars. Reported the *Topeka Weekly Times*, "It seems to be the general opinion that the burned district will be rebuilt at an early day," though only about $30,000 of the loss carried insurance.

In June three years later in Holbrook, Arizona, boys playing in a vacant building with firecrackers started a fire that demolished the town's entire business section with a loss estimated "far up into the thousands." Fanned by gale-force winds, the flames spread so fast down "the long row of business houses and residences which composed the front and practically only street in town." All the buildings' contents were destroyed. News accounts reported, "even the baggage of drummers, the extra clothing of citizens, all their household goods and valuables were but tinder that caught and extended the fierce flames." The conflagration even spread to thirteen railroad cars stranded on an auxiliary track and destroyed their contents. Not a building on the west side of the town remained standing, with only a dozen unscathed residences remaining in the devastated community.

In July 1890 in Howard, South Dakota, a barn fire spread and destroyed the community's two principal business blocks, including the opera house, the newspaper office, and multiple businesses. An elderly couple died in the flames as well. A strong wind from the southwest saved the property on the west side of Main Street, though the buildings were all scorched and their windows shattered from the heat. Reported South Dakota's *Mitchell Capital*, "It is supposed that the fire was started by boys playing near the barn."

A November fire in 1890 Bozeman, Montana, "created considerable excitement all along the business portion of the city" before several hundred men and firefighters rushed to the conflagration in a carpenter shop and stable. The firemen hooked two hoses to the hydrants and doused adjacent buildings with "two strong streams of water" to keep the fire from spreading beyond the one building, which was a total loss estimated at eight hundred dollars. "It is the old story of children playing with matches," reported the *Bozeman Courier*, "and it was fortunate that they escaped destruction themselves."

Besides property damage or demolition, people died due to the accidental arsonists, often the children themselves. Little girls playing with firecrackers in 1897 Pearmount, Montana, exploded several cans of coal oil, killing five-year-old Minnie Nelson. Four-year-old Otis Tosh of Blendville, Missouri, perished when two playmates with matches ignited a barn filled with more than ten tons of hay in 1899. The dress of a four-year-old girl caught fire while she was playing beside a smoldering pile of straw near Watertown, South Dakota, in 1899 with fatal results. Sioux Falls, South Dakota, youngster Oscar Ericson, age four, was playing with an old miner's lamp, which he filled with gasoline and then lit. He lived for five hours after the explosion. In Pleasant Green, Utah, four-year-old Vance Hillman was playing alone when he lit a roman candle and set his clothes on fire. He survived but twenty-seven hours after the accident.

While their parents were absent from their Anaconda, Montana, home in the winter of 1888, the five-year-old daughter and her baby sibling set a curtain on fire while playing with matches. The fire rapidly spread and a neighbor boy rushed into the house, saving the girl but failing to rescue the infant. Boise, Idaho, parents Mr. and Mrs. M.C. Hull in 1899 lost their three-year-old to a blaze caused by children playing with matches. Tragically, it was the Hull's second child lost to an accidental fire.

In the summer of 1877 in Manvel, Dakota Territory, a Norwegian woman with the surname Bokken left her three- and four-year-old children alone while she chased some cattle from her field. When she returned, she found their room on fire. In trying to rescue her offspring, she knocked over a can of kerosene, which ignited and caught her dress on fire. Both children and their mother perished from the blaze. Ruth Jackson, age three of Denison, Texas, was attempting to leap over a blaze she and her playmates had started after piling up weeds and rubbish in a vacant lot. Unfortunately, her dress caught fire, and she was enveloped in flames before her grandmother and uncle could reach her to put out the flames. Little Ruth lived but a few hours after the incident.

Barns were a favorite place for children to play, but a danger when youngsters added matches to their activities. A five-year-old and a seven-year-old died near Brenham, Texas, in 1899 while playing with matches near a pile of cotton. In 1890 Perry, Iowa, Bessie Seeley and Gracie Hall perished after setting a barn ablaze. That same year in Arkansas City, Kansas, a two-year-old died from a barn fire sparked with matches. In Los Angeles in 1896 Hazel and Nonie Bickford, ages three and four, died in their father's barn after playing with matches in the hay.

Assessing the problem in 1876, the *Daily Junction* in Ogden, Utah, observed, "Boys are useful, and so are matches, but they should be kept separate."

Other newspapers printed fire safety rules and precautions. Before Thanksgiving in 1883, the *Montana Record-Herald* of Helena listed nine "timely hints" on fire safety for area residents. Helena Fire Marshal Charles D. Curtis gave the fire safety tips, starting with the first: "Matches should be kept in metal boxes, and where children, rats, and mice cannot meddle with them. If a match or a piece of paper is lighted, see that it is properly extinguished before leaving it, as such will sometimes burst out on fire after having been, as supposed, tramped out."

Curtis further recommended "Parents and guardians are particularly cautioned to watch their children and wards, and not allow them under any circumstances to play with fire or matches. In the past week, two fires were set by children playing with matches; one in a stable and another in a wood shed."

His other recommendations included never leave "candles or lamps burning at a bedside after retiring;" keep fires "as low as comfort will permit," especially on windy days; clean stove flues and chimneys of soot once a month; and fill and trim kerosene lamps by daylight and "when burning keep them out of the draft of open doors and windows."

By the last quarter of the nineteenth century, towns like Helena and others throughout the West created fire departments to help manage the fire danger. In 1888 the Topeka, Kansas, fire department, described by the *North Topeka News* as "a prompt, well-drilled and capable fire department," kept statistics on local fires. The department reported thirty-five fires between April 1 and August 1. Of those blazes, eight or 22.2 percent of all fires were "caused by children playing with matches." The paper reported "the property these children endangered is valued at $3,700, and they succeeded in destroying only $208 worth. Enough to buy books and amusements to last these same children a half decade." Other than matches, kerosene and gasoline were "the most destructive agents in point of the number of fires caused, either directly or indirectly." Gas and kerosene fires were most often caused by overturning a lamp or improperly tending a stove.

Typical of the era's frontier fire departments created to protect local property was that of Abilene, a west Texas community approaching a population of thirty-four hundred. Abilene's municipal fire department employed a chief, two assistants, and fifty-two firemen. In 1897, the department responded to eight alarms, two of them, or twenty-five percent, attributed to boys playing with matches. Two more fires were started by arson, another by a gasoline stove, and three by unknown causes. The department answered those blazes with four horses, two hose carts, a hose wagon, a hook-and-ladder truck, and two thousand feet of cotton hose. In the process, they traveled thirteen miles, laid eight thousand feet of hose, raised nine hundred feet of ladders, and used eight four-gallon extinguishers. Abilene fire losses during 1897 totaled $5,850, "the lightest year yet," according to the *Taylor*

County News. Of that total, insurance covered $3,900, making a net loss of $1,950 on property valued at $90,650.

The *Farmers Leader* in Canton, South Dakota, described the 1896 October loss of a barn filled with two hundred tons of hay and the adjoining stables and sheds as leaving N.H. Thornton "without any food or shelter for his cattle for the winter." Reported the *Leader*, "The usual combination of small boy, match, and haystack resulted in the usual manner in Okoboji."

Accidental fires caused by child play were so common that many times newspapers ascribed conflagrations of unknown causes as "supposed to have been caused by children playing with matches." The 1887 loss of a house and barn in Holland, Texas; the destruction of a residence in 1880 Dallas; the burning of a barn, buggy, cultivator, and corn plow in 1895 Sioux Falls, South Dakota; the destruction of the S.L. Adams smelter in St. George Utah, in 1888; and many other frontier fires were united by that supposition, though it was seldom proved definitively.

Both town and country children were fascinated with matches and wound up creating all sorts of damage and, sometimes, death. Without fire departments and water lines to supply hydrants, conflagrations in rural areas were often the most difficult to control or extinguish. Two boys playing with matches on a farm north of Wichita, Kansas, in 1890 started a fire that burned over twelve square miles of cropland, pasture, and prairie, destroying vast quantities of hay and grain before burning itself out. The loss was estimated at more than $150,000.

Near Pomona, Kansas, in 1895, a structure believed to be the largest private barn in the state was demolished by a fire set by children playing with matches. Clint Burtner's barn was eighty feet wide and a hundred and twenty-five feet long and filled with hay and grain, as well as several valuable animals. All but two horses were saved among the animals, but the grain and hay were destroyed. Wind spread the fire to the Burtner residence, which also burned to the ground, though most of the house's contents were removed and saved. The damage came to more than $7,000 with no insurance to offset even a fraction of the loss.

On the Scott ranch near the abandoned Fort Halleck in Nevada, children and Lucifers destroyed a hundred and fifty tons of hay in 1897. The same cause cost R.D. Towle near Grandview, South Dakota, his barn, a horse, his mower, his hay rake, and other farm machinery, a loss described by the local newspaper as "a serious one to Mr. Towle." A heavy wind fueled an 1891 fire created by children playing with matches near Gary, South Dakota. Mrs. Levi Greely lost her outbuilding, her dwelling, forty tons of hay, and ninety sheep in the conflagration. Reported the *Miller Press*, "Nothing was saved of the household goods. A sleeping infant was barely rescued."

Children burned down the barns and granary of Roger Culhane, south of Aurora, Dakota Territory, in 1884, costing him "all his farm tools, grain, one horse, and eight hogs." West of Newton, Kansas, in 1899, a child with a match set a haystack on fire, which spread to the barn at the Otis Camp place. Fire losses included twenty tons of hay, three hundred bushels of grain, a buggy, a harness, and assorted farm machinery. Reported the local newspaper, "It was only by the hardest kind of work that the house was saved as it was directly in the wind of the burning barn, and several times took fire, but heroic work saved it." A similar barn fire resulting from child play in Washington County, Oregon, in 1896, consumed twenty tons of hay, two hundred bushels of wheat and oats, a buggy, some harnesses, and other farm implements.

The problem of juvenile-spawned fires was serious enough that one Utah paper offered a tongue-in-cheek proposal in 1876. "Why don't parents furnish the boys with nitroglycerine at once?" asked the Ogden *Daily Junction.* "They might do more mischief than with common matches." The paper's facetious suggestion alluded to the fact that more incendiaries than just matches were accessible in frontier communities, especially mining towns where dynamite, blasting caps, and gunpowder were standard commodities. Though few parents would ever have given their children such dangerous materials, children often encountered them in their daily activities.

On an August Sunday afternoon in 1891 San Francisco, an explosion rocked the Holly Park Hill area, breaking windowpanes for a half-mile away and scattered debris in every direction after a tool chest that contained a stick of dynamite exploded. "Boys playing in the vicinity are believed to be responsible for the explosion," according to news accounts. Despite the damage radius, the paper noted the blast hurt no one.

In 1898 El Paso, several boys playing in an alley discovered a blasting cap. Their child-like curiosity drove them to see what it would do, so they put it on a piece of paper, which they lit. They backed away, but not far enough. When the cap exploded, it flung shrapnel and debris at the boys, injuring three with cuts and bruises on their heads and bodies. In Sioux Falls, South Dakota, another set of young lads found and played with a dynamite cap. It exploded in the hand of one, requiring the amputation of two fingers and a thumb. Only the boy's glasses saved his eyes and his sight from shrapnel.

Gunpowder was the most common explosive and children couldn't resist playing with it. In February 1890, two Clark brothers, ages eleven and thirteen, were playing near a powder house when they found some powder. Believing the explosive was damp, the brothers built a fire to dry it out. The ensuing explosion set their clothes on fire. Their mother rushed to them, catching both and throwing them in a nearby pond. According to newspaper reports, "both boys' hands and faces are frightfully burned, and the flesh fell off in large pieces," but both were expected to recover.

In Littleton, Colorado, some boys were playing with a can of gunpowder when one of them lit a match with disastrous results. The 1884 explosion two days before the town's July Fourth celebration burned the face of Charles Donnelly, who lost sight in both eyes. Two of his companions were less seriously injured.

In 1891 in Gallup, New Mexico Territory, little Joe Heine, Jr., suffered burns to his face and arms in an explosion after a playmate tossed a package of gunpowder into a fire. Three years later in Grand Junction, Colorado, youths Fred Campbell and Albert Vial obtained a can of gunpowder from an unknown source and, according to the local *Daily Sentinel*, "not knowing of its deadly nature, they applied a match, with the result that they were both badly burned about the face, hands, and arms."

Two days before the 1896 presidential election between Republican nominee William McKinley and Democratic candidate William Jennings Bryan, a group of Idaho Falls, Idaho, boys "were having a campaign rally," according to newspaper reports. After building a bonfire in the street to show their patriotic fervor, one lad threw a six-pound container of gunpowder into the fire. Poor Willie Pierson's "arm was nearly blown off and his face was burned beyond recognition," according to the news reports.

In Salt Lake City, police officers in January 1899 discovered a group of small boys playing with a "large box of giant powder, which they claim they had found on the street." The police confiscated the dangerous powder. A Utah newspaper reported, "It seems little less than a miracle that the boys did not succeed in blowing themselves and a goodly portion of the neighborhood into eternity."

The DeWitt, Arkansas, community was less fortunate when a container of gunpowder exploded and demolished the store of S.L. Leslie, fatally burning two of his children, injuring the dozen people in the building and damaging thousands of dollars' worth of goods. Newspaper reports indicated, "It is supposed that the explosion was caused by the children playing in the store, who, it is thought, accidentally set fire to a keg of gunpowder."

Childhood curiosity and matches were a dangerous combination on the American frontier, but fire was a common fact of everyday life, necessary for cooking, heating, bathing, and lighting. Households used open hearths, wood-burning stoves, lanterns, and candles, all posing significant dangers to children, whether at work or at play. Among children, burn injuries and accidents were commonplace, both in handling chores such as girls helping with the cooking and laundry or boys tending branding fires or burning brush. Unfortunately, curious children at play with matches often caused more significant injuries and property damage.

The Old West was never a childproof environment. Because survival demanded everyone contribute, children often learned by doing and exploring, even when their curious minds did not always recognize the potential dangers of their actions. Trial-and-error when playing with fire could be fatal. While life on the frontier was full of adventure, it was also replete with danger even in everyday life, especially for children. Matches, kindling, and even black powder, blasting caps and other explosives were often available, and curious youngsters might light a fire just to see what would happen. Frontier survival came at a cost, and childhood, while still filled with wonder, was anything but carefree in the Old West.

While children playing with matches took the blame for many destructive and dangerous fires in the West, children simply playing was actually credited with saving a frontier school outside Elmira, Oregon. A fire started in the woods and dry grass near the Lane County community and rapidly engulfed a nearby farm, where it destroyed the barn. The *St. Helens Mist* newspaper reported, "The fire then spread to the schoolhouse, and came near getting that, but the children playing around the building had worn the grass off some, and the neighbors were able to save it." Thanks to the persistent child play, the hard-packed playground did not provide fuel for the flames to reach the school building.

Chapter Five

Santa and Firecrackers

Holidays on the frontier provided a break from the tedium of daily life in rural areas and offered opportunities for children and their parents to socialize with neighbors they might not see regularly. While Thanksgiving and New Year's presented respite from the routine, the Fourth of July and Christmas remained the two most common and widespread celebrations in the last half of the nineteenth century. The Fourth brought communities together to celebrate the nation's independence and birth, while Christmas united families to rejoice with gifts and food over the birth of Jesus.

Then as today, all children had a recollection of a memorable Christmas, either their first or another that lingered in their memories for decades because of a special present or treat. A Butte, Montana, youth identified only as "Herb" years later looked back on his first as his grandest. "I can remember my first Christmas. They had the tree there and all the little candles on it, just candles. You didn't have any tree lights in those days, and ornaments for the tree were mostly homemade: Strings of popcorn, strings of cranberries, walnuts wrapped in tinfoil.

There'd be a few little ornaments they bought ... One present and a little bag of candy. We were satisfied. It was still Christmas, and we had a big feast."

As the daughter of an army officer, Forrestine Cooper moved from one military post to another during her childhood. She always cherished a poignant and an embarrassing Christmas recollection at two different forts. As a five-year-old at Fort Concho in San Angelo, Texas, Christmas morning 1872 was "vividly impressed upon my memory." She and her little brother, almost three, stood together as their father opened a door into the parlor of their quarters. "We gazed at our first real Christmas tree, decorated with the things that had been sent from Philadelphia for this event," she recalled years later. "I can see that tree distinctly today. Under the tree were two tiny chairs. They were folding chairs with wooden legs and arms of black; white canvas seats; and backs bound with red braid. In one chair was an immense wax doll in a red dress. That was my chair; the other was for my brother."

Forrestine sat in that chair and held her new doll in her arms, thinking Christmas could not get any better, but it did. "At that moment, my mother carried my baby sister into the room and told me I could hold her for a little while." It was the first time she had ever held her newest sibling. "My new sister, Florence, now six weeks old, was not much larger than my new wax doll. These events made that Christmas day stand out very plainly in my memory."

The following year at Fort Sill in Oklahoma Territory, she created another enduring—though not as poignant—memory. It all started a week before Christmas when she returned from play early and walked in on her mother and a female acquaintance in their parlor. The friend held a doll with a china head, legs, and arms. The neighbor was fitting the doll with a ruffled dress trimmed in pink ribbon.

Forrestine rushed to the woman and asked if the doll and dress were for her. The woman replied it was for another little girl at the fort. Disappointed in the response, Forrestine said it was ugly because "it has three eyebrows."

The patient woman said the top mark was the eyebrow, the next mark was the slit where the doll's eyes would open, and the third black line was for the eyelashes. Forrestine said she still did not like "dolls with three eyebrows" and scurried from the room. The next week at the fort-wide Christmas celebration, Forrestine saw the ugly doll again and stood in shock when she learned it was hers. When her mother's friend reminded her it had three eyebrows, Forrestine replied, "Dolls ought to have three eyebrows."

An orphan girl on the Texas frontier, Sarah Harkey in San Saba was left to look after her younger siblings while her two older brothers worked away from their ramshackle cabin to send money to support the family. One year she opened a letter from one brother and found a fifty-dollar bill inside to help with Christmas for his younger siblings. She sobbed with joy. "Here are the children, all barefooted, and the roof lets in the sunshine and rain. I couldn't decide what was best to do." After an estimate for repairing the roof came in at forty dollars or more, "I knew then I would have to give up the idea of repairing, for the children must have shoes and warmer clothes."

Sarah had to borrow a dress from a neighbor to have suitable attire for a trip to town. "We got shoes for all, then jeans for the little boys, pants, and coats, and got my little sister several dresses and myself a worsted dress and a calico dress and material for other purposes and had thirty dollars left. Now I felt independent. I had money to buy food, too. We came home happy." And, Sarah and her brothers and sisters had a merry Christmas despite their leaky roof.

Another Christmas would not turn out as enjoyable for Sarah. After she had married, her husband squirreled away money in a hollowed piece of timber in the house to buy presents for the family Christmas. When he retrieved the pouch he had stuffed with the fifteen one-dollar bills, he discovered rats had eaten his cache of cash. Sarah's Christmas that year was not nearly as merry.

Like Sarah, many pioneer children lived in dire circumstances with little discretionary money to purchase frills such as toys, especially in the early years of the western frontier after the 1849 California Gold Rush. Frontier journalist and author John Hanson Beadle wrote of Christmas in the 1850s out west that "the children in America had to enjoy Christmas with only such sums as they had saved up for months, often a penny at a time." Beadle noted that "save for candy and firecrackers, there was little to spend money for." Writing in 1891 of toys four decades earlier, Beadle noted, "Many a little girl made a doll by dressing up a crook-necked squash. 'Rag babies' were the rule. A doll such as any child of parents above the grade of paupers may now have for Christmas, would then have excited the amazement of the neighborhood, and a doll that would open and shut its eyes—well, language is lacking to set for the furor such a wonderful creation would have excited."

Beadle noted that the 1848 purchase of a two-dollar doll ordered by a westerner from a Cincinnati company "was made the matter of a church discussion" of whether that was an appropriate and moral expenditure. Two dollars in 1848 is the equivalence of almost eighty-one dollars in 2025 money. After the Civil War in 1865, the country entered a second Industrial Revolution, marked by rapid industrial growth and technological advancements.

Not only did these manufacturing innovations make the tools their parents used more effective and less expensive, they also opened up opportunities for mass-produced toys, to the delight of boys and girls throughout the nation. Until then, Beadle reported the children maintained a high regard for craftsmen skilled in whittling figures from wood. "The father who could carve a human-looking figure out of walnut bark," Beadle wrote, "was a hero of his family."

Mass production of inexpensive tin toys diminished the need for the family whittler. Other second Industrial Revolution developments—like plate glass perfected in the middle of the nineteenth century—also affected American Christmases from the big eastern cities to the smallest western towns. Though windows had always been necessary to provide light in stores, the glass panes were small and held in place by muntins, the strips of wood or metal that secured all the panes in a window. With plate glass able to cover a whole store wall facing a sidewalk, windows became not just a light source but also an evolving advertisement for the goods inside. That opened up a new Christmas world for children as merchants put up seasonal displays advertising their wares. Even if their families could not afford many toys, the youngsters could at least see them from the sidewalk and dream of one day receiving them.

By the end of the nineteenth century, stores throughout the country understood the importance of "window shopping," as it was being called. In 1898, for instance, the *Waco Times-Herald* in Texas ran a story "Christmas Show Windows" with the subheadings "Exquisite Displays in Plate Glass Fronts during the Christmas Holidays This Year" and "A Grand Reception for Old Santa Claus." The paper visited merchants in downtown Waco, a town approaching twenty thousand in population, and described their seasonal exhibitions, which not only drew town folks but also rural residents from throughout central Texas. Reported the *Times-Herald*, "It has become a custom in architecture to build first-class storehouses with a special view of giving the occupant large glass windows in which to display his goods. Waco is said to be particularly blessed with show windows."

The paper went on to describe the Christmas displays of more than fifty local merchants, with the most spectacular being that of the Arcade. "There is more genuine joy dispensed at the Arcade than at any one place perhaps in Texas, still it seems to be inexhaustible. It is dispensed not alone to the children. Grown men and women, too, crowd the great toy depot, day and night, and give instructions to be conveyed to Santa Claus."

"The windows of the Arcade," continued the *Times-Herald*, "are full of toys. A tea table, a big doll riding a bicycle, another one in a horseless carriage, trains, cannons, toolboxes, with the national colors for a background, presents a picture that charms everybody. Window No. 2 is also beautiful. A rural scene is presented with cows grazing in the woodland, and a rabbit scampering away. Santa Claus is seen coming full speed, driving his reindeer, and strewing the presents here and there. Above him is another representation of Santa about to drop a doll in a little girl's stocking while she sleeps. Fireworks are plentiful all about, and the average child delights to visit the Arcade."

At China Hall, "A world of toys is displayed in the window of this place, and the children were having a picnic." The Sanger Brothers' display included a diorama of a perplexed Santa Claus scratching his head at a chimney too small and crooked for him to slip through. "The window is very original in conception, and very attractive. Material being used on the floor to represent snow." The diorama was flanked on one side by art pottery, clocks, and dolls, and on the opposite side by toilet sets, workboxes, and case goods.

H.E. Ambold's presentation "always reaches a tender spot in a boy's heart" with its display of rifles, guns, striking-bags, footballs, and other sporting goods." Music dealers Thomas Goggan Brothers "have a very fine display of musical instruments, pianos, violins, guitars, mandolins, tambourines, and accordions." Confectioner J. Prade's front windows were "decorated with homemade fancies. Nuts and bon-bons are also on exhibition, and the place represents a charming appearance." The list went on and on of local merchants and their Christmas displays.

In Grand Junction, Colorado, the Post Office Book and Stationery Store under proprietor F.A. Moore printed a display ad in the *Daily Sentinel*. It read: *"Whoa! Santa Claus!* That's just what we had to say to Santa Claus, and, do you know before we knew it he had dumped (on our store) Boys' Sleds and Wagons, Girls' Dolls, Fancy Cards, Play Blocks, Hobby Horses, Nice Books, Albums, Manicure Sets, Baby Coaches, and the dear knows what all. Oh, Yes! We nearly forgot, a WHOLE TON OF CANDY!"

Elsewhere in La Junta, Colorado, a nine-inch undressed doll could be purchased for a nickel, while a fully attired twenty-inch doll with jointed limbs, natural hair and moving eyes sold for a dollar and ninety-eight cents in 1898.

As early as 1881, William Beck & Son in Portland, Oregon, was advertising itself as "Santa Claus Headquarters" with a vast stock of mechanical toys, wax dolls, rubber toys, French dolls, games, rocking horses, and bicycles.

By the 1890s, newspapers across the country were running messages to Santa — some cute, some funny, and many poignant. In 1888 the *Austin American-Statesman* observed, "The custom of sending letters to Santa Claus, asking him for certain coveted gifts is becoming more general every year," then gave an example of one such letter that had reached their office. "Dear Old Man: I want an ox whip to slash the stuffin' out of our Billy goat, who bucks me over, a brass cannon, and a gun to scare Jim with. Don't put my things in Jim's stockings. My stockings are red, with holes in the knees. Ma and Pa are always foolin' about Christmas Eve, but come along and don't mind them. Yours, Tom. "P.S. I don't like peppermint sticks."

By 1899 the U.S. Post Office in the nation's capital reported, "From the increased number of letters addressed to Santa Claus received at the dead letter office this year, it is evident that the popular illusion of childhood has as strong a hold as ever." The report noted that the dead letter office had received more than a thousand such letters in December, with the most frequently requested items being dolls and candy. Some letters arrived without stamps and some with two-cent stamps. Others showed up with nickel stamps, leading Post Office officials to speculate the senders were "evidently laboring under the impression that the supposed dispenser of toys resided in some foreign country which was a member of the international postal union." The mail service, in typical bureaucratic style, noted, "Where the address of the sender is given, the letters are returned; otherwise they are destroyed."

In Oregon, two little girls did not trust the Post Office to deliver their messages to the jolly fellow so they "have been in the habit every Christmas of writing letters to Santa Claus and burning them in the grate in order that he might get them at the top of the chimney."

The *Evening World-Herald* in Omaha, Nebraska, reported on December 21, 1898, that Santa Claus was very busy before Christmas and did not have time to read letters, but as a subscriber to the paper, he always took a break after breakfast to read the children's letters published in the newspaper. One such letter from Daisy Davis of 3858 Seward Street stated, "Dear Santa Claus: I don't want you to forget me. I would like a little piano, a washboard, and tub, so I can help grandma wash, a nice book, a pair of mittens, a bottle of perfume, a doll, and lots of good things to eat, and a doll carriage. Bring me all of these you can."

The *Pine Bluff Daily Graphic* in Arkansas also claimed Santa Claus as a regular and careful reader who "will no doubt give what the children have to say his earnest consideration." Floy Herring of 1519 West Sixth Avenue in Pine Bluff published in the newspaper this letter: "Dear Santa Claus: Will you please be so good and kind and bring me a pretty dress, hat, and jacket for Xmas, and a pair of shoes and long stockings, and fill them full of nuts and nice pretty things, and a doll and pretty little cup and saucer. Now, dear Santa, don't forget me. I will go to bed early and sleep tight, and not watch you 'til daylight. I am a good little girl, six years old."

The *Slater Missouri Index* encouraged children to send the newspaper their letters to Santa Claus under certain conditions: "Must be written on one side of the paper. Must be brief. Must be written by little boys and girls not over ten years of age." Judges would determine the best letters, and the little boy writing the selected missive would receive a "handsome suit of clothes" from Walton's Big Store, and the little lass penning the top letter would get "a pretty doll" from J.B. Land.

In 1890s Kansas, Mabel King wrote, "Dear Santa Claus: I will write you and tell you that I have moved; I am not living in Wichita anymore. I live a mile and a quarter from Dighton. Now I will tell you what I want for Christmas. I would like to have two yards of blue ribbon, a silk handkerchief, a pair of kid gloves, a gold ring with a blue set in it, a gold bracelet and a mackintosh. I think I will have a good time Christmas."

James McClelland, in his letter to Santa, got right to the point. "I want a ball, an orange, a knife, a top, a watch, and a sack of candy."

Young Kansan Lyle McKinnis wrote, "Dear Santa Claus: I think you will soon be coming with your jingle, jingle bells, oh! I can hardly wait; it's so many days before you get here; please don't send your wife; me want a surely Santa this time. Please bring me lots of stuff for boys, a hammer, some nails, a ball, a French harp, a slingshot, a drum, a sack of nuts, four bushels of candy, an orange as large as the moon, and a watch with some wheels in it, well bye-bye."

Or, there was this poignant letter from another Kansan: "I is a little girl just seven years old. My name is Perl Moony. Please, Santy, give me a doll and some candy and a watch. I got no papa."

Beulah Arbogast was thinking of her Kansas neighbors when she wrote, "Dear Santa Claus: I am a little girl ten years old. I wanted to write you a letter this year, but I am not expecting much this year, for I would rather see the poor children get toys than myself. But I am rather expecting a doll, which is one of my favorite playthings. I will close now, hoping to see you at Christmas."

Little Beulah Lindsay asked for a doll, a ring, candy, nuts, gum, two handkerchiefs and a friendship heart engraved with Santa's initials. She concluded her Pleasanton, Kansas, letter with, "I wish I had something to send you, but as you manufacture so many pretty things, I wouldn't know what to give you."

Susan Brown added a postscript to Santa in her missive: "I live in the southwest part of town in a yellow house. I think you know it. I will have my stocking ready for you."

Roy Woods provided Santa with an extensive list for himself and his sister. "I wish you would send me a horn, a drum, a little jumping jack, a sack of candy, a top, a doll for my little sister, a knife for me, a box of crayons, a sack of candy for my little sister, a little horse, and wagon, a little barn, a ball, and bat, a slate and pencil, a tablet, a mouth harp, a set of dishes for my little sister, a stove, a pair of glasses and sewing machine for my little sister; my little sister lives out in the country, a coat and vest and pants, a pencil box, a pair of knee pads, a handkerchief, a flag, a necktie, a pair of suspenders, a knife and fork and plate for sister, a cap for me and a dress for sister."

By contrast, Johnnie Wells in the same edition of the *Dighton Herald* made a simple request to Santa: "Please bring me whatever you will, and I will be satisfied."

In Oklahoma City, the Weiser sisters both wrote to Santa Claus, perhaps with a little help from their mother. Wrote Nellie Weiser, "Dear Mr. Santie: If you would bring me that little stove, I will leave you a great big popcorn ball on the table. Oh! Santie, I prayed last night, and my sister prayed for you to bring me that stove. Goodbye, Santie."

Her sister Edith echoed Nellie's request. "Dear Mr. Santie: Please send my sister Nellie that little stove in Mr. Wand's drug store. Last night when I said my prayers, I asked Jesus to please tell you to send my sister that stove. She wants it so bad. My name is Edith. I am five years old, and sister Nellie is seven. Goodbye, Santie, and send me something good."

Young John in Salinas, California, wrote, "Dear Santa Claus: My ma told me to write to you. Please bring me a gun and a pair of rubber boots. If you can't spare them both, please, I'll take the gun. I don't mind if I do get my feet wet."

A young farm boy, who lived outside Newell, Arkansas, wrote St. Nick with a list of gifts he sought and some safety instructions. "Dear Santy Claus: I am a little country boy. Christmas will soon be here, and I will write you so you will get my letter in time to come see me. Please bring me some firecrackers, some oranges, apples, a coconut, and candy, and a pistol and caps. My little dogs, Jack and Lee, won't bite you. Don't bring your goat in the lot. My goat will butt him over and might break your cart. I will cover the fire up so you won't burn your feet when you come down the chimney. I will go to bed early. Your friend, Charley Cooper."

Seven days before Christmas in 1891, the *Omaha World-Herald* printed a letter from a young boy of 1120 Arbor Street, asking Santa to "please bring me a few toys. I never had a Christmas present only once, and that was when I was three years old, so please bring me a few this Christmas. I will remember you if you do. I cannot say much this time because I am sick. But please bring me some toys. My mother and father are poor, and so am I. Well, Santa, I have not much to say. Goodbye. Your loving friend, John Hinchey."

Another indigent child wrote a letter that the *San Francisco Call* ran in December 1899. "Dear Santa Claus: I am a little girl, six years old. I go to school (and) am in the second grade ... I have two brothers. I don't know whether you will come to see us this Christmas or not. Mama says we are too poor, but I think you will come cause we can't help being poor. Hoping to see you Christmas and wishing you a merry Xmas and a fine trip. I am your little friend, Lillian Jones, Clipper Gap, Placer County, California."

While Christmas was a worldwide holiday to be celebrated, the Fourth of July was solely an American holiday. John Taylor Waldorf in Virginia City, Nevada, remembered how he and his friends viewed the annual calendar because they liked to make noise. "We split our year into two days, and have a heap more noise, 'cause one is Christmas and the other's Fourth of July." While a few families celebrated Christmas with firecrackers, most families exploded them to celebrate the nation's Day of Independence in a flurry of patriotic activities. The squeals of delight on Christmas morning were replaced on July Fourth with the sounds of exploding fireworks, marching bands, patriotic speeches, and noisy competitions to the great delight of youngsters.

"Fourth of July was a day of early rising," Waldorf recalled. "We used to get up before the sun lit up the streets, but not before the beams had begun to caress the flag on Mount Davidson. The splendor that the Stars and Stripes borrowed from heaven made our hearts beat with a fierce patriotism and filled us 'chock full' of a brand of enthusiasm that meant trouble for the timid, nervous folk who dreaded redheads, bombs, and double-headed Dutchmen [types of firecrackers]."

Adjacent to Virginia City, the community of Gold Hill, Nevada, joined in the festivities as well. Reported the *Gold Hill Daily News* in 1868, "A much finer day for the celebration of the 'ever glorious Fourth,' than we enjoyed last Saturday, could barely have been vouchsafed to the people of Gold Hill and Virginia [City]. All the night before, premonitory symptoms of fun to come were heard in the occasional popping of crackers, firing of pistols, and the execution of such like ambitious noises.... At an early hour flags and streamers were displayed from the flagstaffs of mining works, prominent institutions, across the streets, and in fact every place where such could be expected, and

'Old Glory' floated proudly in the morning sun from the new flagstaff on the lofty pinnacle of Mount Davidson."

The paper continued, "Virginia being settled upon for the great parade, assumed quite the stirring appearance. Firemen and soldiers were hurrying to their respective rendezvous, and the ladies on the balconies, the little girls and boys, everybody were arrayed in their best holiday attire. Wagons after wagons, too, rolled in from the country around, loaded with men, women, and children, coming to see the parade and the general fun, and all bearing the national colors, even the horses being decked with little flags. The quantity of firecrackers and other fulminating compounds of villainous saltpeter and tough paper noisily consumed during the day was enormous, as usual on such occasions, and both old and young America were in the height of patriotic felicity."

The combined Virginia City-Gold Hill parade boasted numerous bands, several fraternal organizations, and floats or wagons, featuring little girls dressed as the Goddess of Liberty and little boys wearing costumes of Revolutionary War soldiers.

"Crack! Bang! Boom!" is how the *Spokane Chronicle* described that Washington city's 1898 festivities during the Spanish-American War. The paper's afternoon edition observed, "This is the Fourth of July, and all day long, firing everything from the smallest firecracker to the heaviest anvils has proclaimed the patriotism of Spokane people and the joy of the brave boys in Cuba. It has been many years since the people have had such a special cause for national rejoicing on Independence Day as they have this year, and they are making the most of it. The Fourth of July orations all over the country have more of the old-style ring, the Declaration of Independence was read with more spirit, and the 'Star-Spangled Banner' was sung with more enthusiasm than since the days of the Civil War."

The *Chronicle* noted that the celebration began well before midnight with premature fireworks. "Some of the enthusiasts could not resist the temptation to begin the firing of salutes yesterday and especially yesterday evening."

In 1886 in Kansas, the *Abilene Journal* noted the impact of the celebration on children by writing, "The glorious Fourth of July is chiefly enjoyed to its fullest extent among the rising generation, the boys and girls. Unlucky and disgraced, indeed, is the boy who, at the end of the bombardment of the day, has got off without a powder burn, or a shot finger, or even his toggery unsinged. Probably the greatest hero is the boy who not only has, with his toy pistol, carelessly and adroitly winged another boy, but who, in the melee, has also been able to do what is by no means a rare feat—wound himself with his own weapon, for many a grown-up man has foolishly looked down the muzzle of a gun, and the generous spirit of the boys is shown by the greater number of times in which they shoot themselves instead of others. The boys and girls who get up with the lark, and are on a lark all the day, and keep up the lark until the night shades are falling; what a glorious time they will have! It is the capping climax, the kernel of the nut of delight—the greatest of the great joys of the Fourth of July."

The *Journal* then described the incendiary celebration: "The squares and streets become alive with burning fire of all the colors of the rainbow, lighted by the smoldering fuse held by every boy and girl, while, rising higher and higher the skyrocket cleaves the dark heavens and fills the sky with more radiant and varied colored stars and comets than can ever be seen, even on a clear starlight night. The incessant rattle of musketry coming from the burning, crackling bunches of exploding firecrackers, with the heavy flash of light sparks as the skyrocket flies from its prison, the exquisite pleasures of the wildly revolving spinning wheels, and the noise as of a clap of thunder, which makes the boys and girls tremble, clinging to each other or their mothers, and hiding their faces in their dresses, as an immense pot of powder shoots up into the dark night air, displaying its lovely bouquet of flowers, while every face radiates with joy in the suddenly and beautifully illuminated night darkness, add to the fascinations of the glorious night."

An account in the *Sheridan County Democrat* in Hoxie, Kansas, estimated one-and-a-half-million dollars' worth of fireworks were imported, primarily from China, into the United States annually. Three-fourths of those imports were used to celebrate the Fourth of July, largely on account of a letter American patriot and future president John Adams wrote to his wife. On July 3, 1776, Adams penned a note to his beloved Abigail, writing, "I am apt to believe that [Independence Day] will be celebrated by succeeding generations as the great anniversary festival. It ought to be commemorated as the day of deliverance, by solemn acts of devotion to God Almighty. It ought to be solemnized with pomp and parade, with shows, games, sports, guns, bells, bonfires, and illuminations [fireworks], from one end of this continent to the other, from this time forward forevermore."

But a hundred and eleven years later, not everyone was so sure about the noisy celebration, as articulated by the *Times* of Clay Center, Kansas, on July 5, 1887. "Who started this combination of youth and saltpeter, of vocal haircloth and the limbs of the jumping jack, of fire, fizzle, and bang? It is laid at John Adams' door because he said something about the ringing of bells, the firing of cannon, etc. But could he have taken the small boy into account when he said it? Did he dream of the annual nerve-racking tumult he was preparing for future generations? Had he any idea that Fourth of July celebrations would so generally be carried on, or at least aggravated, by small boys of extraordinary lung power and never-faltering energy? Impossible! John Adams was a noble man, a patriot, a statesman, but he was not in all things a clairvoyant. He could not look forward and see the small boy of 1887 celebrating the Fourth of July to the terror and peril of his seniors. The toy pistol was not in vogue in John Adams' day, nor had the firecracker obtained a foothold on American soil. Dogs with explosives tied to their tails entered not Mr. Adams' idea of celebrating. All these have come in with other modern implements of torture until we now have a day which powder and the small boy claim for their own."

Three years before the *Times* of Clay Center outlined the problem with boys and firecrackers, the merchants of Hawthorne, Nevada, opted not to sell the noisemakers before the 1884 celebration. Reported the town's *Walker Lake Bulletin*, "The Fourth of July was a successful Fourth. The weather was just right, and nothing was wanting to make everything pleasant. A distinguishing feature was the absence of noise. While all enjoyed themselves to their utmost, including, of course, the usual amount of patriotic beverages, there was not the average amount of drunkenness. Another great improvement on all previous anniversaries was the freedom from the pest of firecrackers and Chinese bombs. A few, of course, were heard, but the disagreeable racket was missing, and the merchants received a silent vote of thanks from the citizens for not providing the destroying Chinese fireworks for the amusement of the children and the annoyance and tribulation of property owners."

In 1896 Chloride, New Mexico, folks gathered at noon to hear patriotic "recitations and readings" before enjoying a "bountiful repast ... served by the ladies." After the meal, "a glorious downpour of rain occurred, promptly checking any further attempt at holiday making" and dampening the festivities, including any fireworks.

In 1899 La Junta, Colorado, five thousand people gathered to celebrate the Fourth, marking "the greatest crowd ever assembled in the county seat." Crowed the *Tribune*, "From the firecracker's first crack at early dawn to the fizz-wheel's last fizz at the fireworks display, La Junta's Fourth of July celebration was a grand success." After the parade, a community barbecue fed more than three thousand La Junta and Otero County citizens over the ensuing three hours. The children and adult diners consumed eight hundred and thirty pounds of beef, two hundred hams, three hundred pounds of bologna sausage, fifteen hundred onions, two thousand radishes, two barrels of pickles, twelve hundred and fifty loaves of bread, and fifty gallons of coffee. Afternoon activities included a patriotic baseball game where the La Junta youngsters "walloped the kid team of Las Animas … to the tune of thirty-three to twelve." Other afternoon events included bicycle races, tugs of war, greased pig contests, sack races, burro races, greased pole climbing, and foot races, among others.

La Junta's "celebration concluded with a grand display of fireworks on Trinidad plaza. The display was cut short by an unfortunate accident in which about one-half of the fireworks went up in a promiscuous blaze of glory."

In Texas the *Abilene Semi-Weekly Farm Reporter* the day after the 1889 celebration wrote, "The occasion was observed in a quiet way by almost everybody, while the hilarious small boy, with his fireworks, toy pistol, tin can and dog was on hand with his old-time promptness to remind the citizens that the heart of young America still glowed with that patriotic sentiment, which has made it distinguished on this earth." The farm journal continued,

"The Fourth of July is an occasion that should always be observed when possible. It should be talked of in the home circle, on the streets, and in the schoolrooms. Children should be taught to understand its meaning and the purpose of its observance, that the patriotism, which ushered in this glorious day, may be kept alive for all time to come. This is, in many respects, the most remarkable day in the history of the world. The success of the Declaration of Independence has changed the theory of government in nearly all civilized countries."

An 1899 hot air "balloon ascension and double parachute jump" highlighted the celebration in North Seattle, though a fire caused by "a small boy" throwing a firecracker in Spangenberg's Cutlery store and igniting a box of fireworks disrupted the parade when fire department members in the procession abandoned the festivities to do their jobs. The celebrating firemen put out the fire to the delight of "thousands of people on the street." The loss amounted to three hundred dollars.

Two little boys playing with firecrackers at Tower City, Dakota Territory, set fire to the grass near the grain elevator in 1883, "and a disastrous conflagration was averted only by the most strenuous exertions of the citizens," noted the *Yankton Press and Dakotan*.

The *Blackfoot News* in Idaho reported, "The great Fourth of July, 1895, has gone floating forever down the River of Time. It was a great day in Blackfoot. Every preparation was promptly met by the different committees, and the well-selected program was rendered to the letter. The town was at its best in patriotic displays of bunting and flags, and every citizen caught inspiration from the scene. The day was ushered in with the roar and rattle of guns. At an early hour, people were pouring in from the country in all directions at a way evident that a large crowd would be in attendance."

Blackfoot activities included "a declamation contest," a formal speaking competition where children recited famous speeches, literary passages, or original compositions, and were judged on delivery, emotion, and articulation. Such contests were a staple of public education on the American frontier in local academies and during lyceum gatherings across the country. For children under twelve, Hamilton Wright finished first and Georgia Hammond took second. For competitors between the ages of twelve and sixteen, Thomas G. Bond placed first and Vinnie Wilder claimed second place. Prizes of five dollars went to the first-place recipients and of two dollars and fifty cents to the second-place contestants. By contrast, children's prizes in the athletic competitions—sack race, foot races at various distances, jumping contests and other competitions—topped out at a dollar. On this day, patriotism was valued more than athleticism.

Similar Fourth competitions were held in nearby Boise and in frontier communities across the west. The Boise activities included the normal foot races as well as a pin-the-tail-on-the-donkey competition for boys and girls, with Alfred Girard winning the five-dollar purse. The Boise celebration also boasted a contest for the "handsomest lady on the grounds" won by Bertha Gasser along with a ten-dollar prize and for "ugliest man on the grounds" claimed by Daniel Bacon along with the two-dollar-and-fifty-cent reward.

While firecrackers caused a lot of noise, periodic damage, regular injuries, and occasional fatalities, one pioneer always spoke on the Fourth of July about how firecrackers had actually saved his life. As a young man, S.B. Pillsbury was working with a surveying party in southwest Kansas when he was sent back to the crew's supply station thirty miles distant to restock their provisions. On the return trip with two loaded pack mules, he was attacked by a band of a dozen Apache Indians.

To defend himself, he shot his two mules to hide behind as the marauders charged. He held them off with a rifle and a shotgun, knocking a couple off their horses until they retreated to regroup. Knowing he stood little chance of surviving another assault, Pillsbury remembered the "dozen bunches of firecrackers" he had packed for a prairie celebration of the upcoming Fourth. He retrieved the fireworks, shortened the fuses, built a small fire of twigs and grass, and waited for the attack.

"The rush came. I led with my rifle and threw the crackers into the fire. I pumped both barrels of buckshot into the Apaches, and the crackers set up a roar like a platoon of musketry. The Indians were astounded and, dividing to the right and left, went by me like the wind." They never returned, and Pillsbury had an early life-saving Fourth of July celebration he would never forget.

The 1879 Rapid City celebration in Dakota Territory began at the break of day with the Rapid City battery "firing salutes, and continued discharging guns each minute until an earth-shaking discharge for every state and five for the Territory of Dakota had been given," reported the *Black Hills Weekly Journal*. "Aside from the breaking of a few panes of glass by the tremendous concussions, no accident attended the cannonading. By seven o'clock all the residents, and such of the visitors as had arrived the night before, were on the streets, and wagons, gaily decorated with miniature flags, commenced to pour in from the mountains and lower valley, and the national colors were waving from many business houses and a number of private residences—majestically streaming out to the breeze above them all being the splendid banner which floated from the lofty liberty pole in front of *The Journal* office."

Many towns equated Adams' suggestion to celebrate with guns as a directive to fire off big guns like cannons. Few frontier towns had cannons, so the locals started the odd practice of "firing anvils." Anvils were heavy iron or steel implements with a flat top and a tapered end used by blacksmiths to hammer, shape, and forge hot metal into horseshoes, iron tools, wagon wheel rims, and other metallic frontier necessities. Standard blacksmith shop anvils weighed between a hundred and twenty-five pounds and a hundred and fifty pounds.

Citizens in communities without a ceremonial cannon would take two anvils to the middle of a street or vacant lot and position a base anvil on the ground, then pour a dose of gunpowder either in a hole atop the implement or spread the explosive on the flat surface. After positioning a fuse in the powder, the celebrants turned the top anvil upside down and lowered it over the base anvil.

When all was set, somebody lit the fuse and waited for the powder to detonate. When it did, the explosion propelled the upper anvil skyward, sometimes more than fifty feet in the air. The boom was impressive, as was the ensuing flight, though the landing could be tough on anyone who failed to get out of the way. It was a celebratory ritual that drew crowds and applause, mixing patriotism, spectacle, and danger in the grand spirit of nineteenth-century celebration. In 1894 Shiner, Texas, the local newspaper reported, "The glorious Fourth was ushered in this morning by the firing of anvils, and the town was treated to another false fire alarm." Eventually, many communities banned the practice of firing anvils as too dangerous for public safety.

The *El Paso Herald* during the height of the Spanish-American War in 1898 gave a rousing account of the border city's celebration. "Bands were playing all the morning, and gaily dressed horses and bicycles sped through the streets carrying men and women, boys and girls, who were making ready to celebrate the Fourth of July in a way never before attempted here. Evidences on every hand demonstrated that the people were roused as they had not been in a generation.... At an early hour, the people of El Paso began to throng the streets to see the procession. By the hour of nine, it was very near impossible to get through the masses of humanity. Girls had on white gowns and enough red, white, and blue ribbon to show in pretty fashion the patriotism that stirred their hearts. Parades are generally late, but this one was not." The *Herald* noted that the biggest treat on that hot July day was the free ice water provided by a local ice company and a water agent.

One Independence Day celebration reflecting the changing times occurred in 1883 in Yankton, Dakota Territory, when a contingent of Sioux took part in the parade, drawing curious settlers—adults and children alike—to see the indigenous tribe just seven years after the Battle of the Little Big Horn. Reported the *Yankton Press and Dakotan* in language common to the time, "The procession moved slowly down the streets in the order given, bands playing and colors playing. The Indian end of the cavalcade was the object of general interest. There were fully a hundred savages in line, stripped to their breechcloths, their bodies daubed with yellow and red paint and streaked with artistic touches, which gave contrasting colors. Their legs and arms were ornamented with bands and feathers and bells, and their heads were decked with extravagant collections of feathers and quills. As the procession moved through the streets, the Indians danced to the music of their drums and filled the air with blood-curdling whoops. It was a strange, fantastic scene—one which civilization seldom witnesses."

The newspaper report continued, "The Indians entered into the spirit of the occasion with savage ardor and appeared to enjoy in its fullest sense the opportunity to exhibit their barbaric customs. They were not sham Indians, but wild Sioux from the plains, and all the wild instincts of their people were fully demonstrated in their conception and execution of the part assigned them. Accompanying the cavalcade were hundreds of Indians, children, and squaws, who did not participate actively in the honors of the day. Some of these were mounted, but the majority were on foot."

Concluded the *Yankton Press and Dakotan*, "The truth is that the Indians were the principal feature of yesterday's celebration."

Just as Christmas drew families together, the Fourth of July drew Americans together, even those who had once been enemies on the frontier. The children who witnessed the 1883 parade in Yankton took away memories that would last a lifetime, just as they remembered that one special Christmas that would stay with them forever.

Chapter Six

Big Tops and Footlights

Not even Christmas Day could rouse John Taylor Waldorf from his bed at two o'clock in the morning, but the annual arrival of the circus train in Virginia City, Nevada, was a different matter altogether. Waldorf and his friends arose early and willingly on circus day when on any other morning it "would require at least three calls and the threat of a 'dose of strap oil' to make me crawl out from under the covers."

And why not? The circus provided an entertaining escape from daily hardships, much like the frontier theater, but much more exciting, as it combined the elements of an art exhibit, a traveling zoo, a professional band, a parade, a sideshow with oddities, a gymnastic meet with acrobats and aerialists, an equestrian show, a fashion show with performers and animals in exotic costumes, an occasional history lesson, and a three-ring environment awhirl with amazing activities and prankish clowns.

"Several thousand people are in the city from neighboring towns and from the country," proclaimed the *Evening Kansan* of Newton in May 1897. "Circus day is equal to any legal holiday of the year, and today might have been a legal holiday so far as appearances were concerned. Nothing is quite of so much interest to everybody as a circus."

The spectacle offered children a brief glimpse of the world beyond the boundaries of their farms or small communities. A circus was a childhood delight, allowing frontier youngsters to see exotic animals like elephants, lions, tigers, camels, zebras, monkeys, and even an occasional rhinoceros, giraffe, or hippopotamus.

To fill that need for rural entertainment, a variety of circuses roamed the West from the end of the Civil War until the turn of the century. Among the more notable ones were Lee and Ryland's Circus in the 1860s; Howe's Great London Circus, Chiarini's Royal Italian Circus, Jackley's Vienna Circus, and Montgomery Queen's California Circus in the 1870s; Cole's Circus, Sells Brothers Circus, Grand Circus Royal and English Menagerie, Barnum, and Bailey's Circus, and Colonel Wood's Circus in the 1880s; and Wallace's Circus, Adam Forepaugh Circus, Bond Brothers Circus, and Ringling Brothers Circus in the 1890s. When the circus reached town, it captured the fascination of all, the children, especially.

"With us, the circus began with the arrival of the wonderful canvas-covered trains and the unloading of the animals," Waldorf remembered of his Virginia City childhood. "The boy who was denied this pleasure was the object of mingled pity and contempt, and we used to say of him, 'Aw, he might as well be a girl'."

Whether boys or girls, frontier children could not miss the "art exhibit" plastered around town and on country barns in the weeks leading up to the circus's arrival. Advance agents swathed buildings with handbills, posters, and advertisements, all with bright, eye-catching colors bursting with visual excitement to dazzle everyone's eyes and senses. Advance men would blanket towns with their promotional materials, pasting them on barns, fences, saloon entrances, store windows, depot platforms, and even outhouses. Illustrations featured exotic animals like roaring lions, leaping tigers, or parading elephants and performers like trapeze artists frozen in midair mid-leap, trick riders standing atop their galloping steeds, or clowns surrounded by laughing children. Because of their bright colors of reds, yellows, blues, oranges, and greens, the artwork stirred the imaginations of youngsters and adults alike.

Besides distributing flyers, the advance team also purchased newspaper ads to promote the upcoming performances and their phenomenal stars and acts. In short, circus advertising in the Old West was the 19th-century equivalent of a multimedia campaign—a riot of color, motion, and fantasy meant to seduce the imagination and increase local anticipation long before the first wagon or train car reached town.

Assessing the impact of the images, the *Wise County Messenger* in Decatur, Texas, in 1889, observed, "The flaming bills displayed on the walls, and fences and on the ends of country barns, possess for the average juvenile a sort of magic that nothing in the world holds for him. The camelopards (giraffes) as high as a house, and the lions the size of the broadside of a barn, and the bareback riders turning their heels over their heads and putting their feet in their mouths, and the trapeze performers hanging by their toes in midair, and jumping through hoops, are full of attraction for the boys, and for some of the pretty old boys, too, if we may judge by the way they stop and study the advertisements."

Once the train or wagon caravan reached the outskirts of town, packs of boys and an occasional girl gathered to watch the unloading of animals or to offer their services hoping to get to water an elephant or to earn a free pass to a circus performance from a circus teamster, tent man, menagerie man, wagon man, or roustabout. Noted a Salina, Kansas, newspaper in 1899, "An army of several hundred boys is always present at the unloading of a circus. They are nearly always in the way, and it is a wonder more are not hurt than are. The showmen are not so bad a lot as many think and are always ready to give the 'kids' a job, remunerating them with a pass into the circus."

"We spent hours of joy watching the circus hands transferring that precious freight to the platform," Waldorf recalled of Virginia City's circus days. "We looked over the horses with a critical eye and chose the ones that pleased us most. It didn't matter that we got no bill of sale. They were ours for the moment. We followed the last of the cages down to the circus grounds and watched the tents go up before we remembered that we hadn't had any breakfast, and we wouldn't have thought of it then if the circus cooks hadn't begun to get busy with pots and pans.

"Then we ran home, bolted down a few bites and a cup of coffee, grabbed a 'hunk' of bread in each hand, smeared the bread with jelly, and did the rest of our breakfasting as we ran back to the circus grounds. That was the annual experience," Waldorf recalled with fondness years later.

The *El Paso Times* described the popular draw of the circus in October 1887: "Every train that arrived yesterday brought a mass of humanity to see the show, while every wagon road was lined with vehicles of all descriptions." The paper also reported that the school superintendent let students out in the morning to see the parade, "but he gave notice that the presence of the circus would not be taken as an excuse for absence (in the afternoon), consequently the school was not depopulated to any extent."

"So much greater was the attendance at the circus than school this afternoon," reported the 1883 *Union County*

Courier in Elk Point, Dakota Territory, "as to cause the school to dismiss for half a day." The paper went on to report, "Some say the circus was very good while others pronounced it very bad. Perhaps both are incorrect versions."

At most stops, a morning parade from the edge of town or the railroad depot to the circus grounds preceded performances to whet local appetites for the entertainment and wonders that awaited them—for the price of a ticket— later in the afternoon and evening. Regarding the Sells Brothers Circus, the *Leavenworth Times* in 1882 Kansas noted, "There were features in the parade to please everybody. The herds of elephants and dromedaries struck the lover of natural history; the splendid horses suited the taste of the liverymen; the jack-in-the-box people on top of the cages made the young people laugh; the music from several bands pleased the ear of the street audience; the richly decorated wagons suited the eye of the artist; and the clowns made everybody happy."

In 1899, the *National Field* of Salina, Kansas, reported, "Early this morning the streets of the city showed varied scenes of activity, and by nine o'clock farmers with their families could be seen coming in crowds from every direction. It is a gala day for Salina. Nearly everybody came downtown to witness the parade, which was the best ever seen here."

The *Argus-Leader* described the 1897 Ringling Brothers parade this way: "At ten the street display was under way, and it is entirely conservative to say that never in the history of Sioux Falls has so imposing a show been made. Twelve blocks were covered with brilliant chariots, open cages, exhilarating bands, magnificent horses, huge elephants, awkward camels, screeching steam piano and loud-tone chimes of bells, gaily caparisoned equestrians, and all the other elements which go to make up a great circus parade."

Of special interest to the children were the allegorical floats and tableau wagons painted with gaudy illustrations of popular fables such as Mother Goose, Little Red Riding Hood, Jack the Giant Killer, and other childhood tales. Some wagons carried cages of baby lions, baby tigers and other exotic animal young.

While the parade occupied the locals with visions of the thrills to come, roustabouts and canvas men worked on setting up the big top and preparing for matinee and evening performances. Other circus employees included the elite performers and the ring attendants, who helped set up before the performance and kept the show running once it began. After the setup was completed, the hands took on secondary jobs as ticket sellers, ushers, and vendors. Tickets generally sold for a dollar for adults and fifty cents for children under ten.

A small traveling circus like the gaudily named Stoddard's Circus and Great Zoological Exposition, which visited Tombstone, Arizona, in 1879, entered town with four wagons, preceded by four horsemen and followed by two more riders with perhaps fifty circus performers and workers. The circus grounds featured little more than a single tent and cages for the circus animals. The ballyhooed menagerie included a single elephant, a tiger, two Mexican mountain lions, a pair of well-trained monkeys, two parrots and "a lazy alligator in a pool of stinking water," according to a newspaper account.

By contrast, a large operation like the Ringling Brothers Circus arrived by train in Newton, Kansas, in 1897, and set up its temporary home on a twelve-acre plot of ground near the railroad roundhouse. At the center of the grounds stood the "big top," a massive canvas enclosure four hundred and thirty-six feet long by two hundred and twenty-five feet wide. That same year in Sioux Falls, South Dakota, the Ringling Brothers Circus arrived in town with sixty-five railroad cars split among five separate trains with approximately a thousand circus employees handling the myriad of tasks necessary to manage the arrival, setup, performance, takedown, and departure.

The Ringling Brothers' extensive 1890s menagerie—in contrast to the meager Stoddard animal collection—included between sixteen and twenty-five elephants as well as lions, tigers, leopards, boas, hippopotamuses, monkeys, camels, bears, domestic and foreign horses, and other beasts from around the globe.

Not only did children thrill at seeing the exotic animals before the show, they also saw dramatic animal and human feats once the performances began under the canvas big top. Smaller circuses would have only one ring filled with activity, but many of the larger outfits like Ringling Brothers and their Barnum and Bailey competitor managed three rings with a dizzying array of activities that overwhelmed the senses of young ones and adults alike.

"The big canvas amphitheater," observed the Newton, Kansas, newspaper, "is such a maze of aerial paraphernalia and circus rigging that is a bewildering sight of itself, but when no less than twenty performers are at work in the three rings and two stages at one moment, it is impossible to see the half that is being done. Therefore, although one pair of eyes cannot be expected to see everything, yet there is just as much for every pair of eyes to see as the eyes have the capacity to take in." A Salina paper noted, "There was not a dull moment, and the score of clowns enlivened the program with their many capers and frolics."

Various circuses promoted such acts as "a horse that walks a tight rope;" high flying trapeze artists; trick riders; trained dog acts; tumblers, and jugglers; a Persian aerialist;

a family posing as statues; jugglers; strong men; high-wire specialists; wild animal performances; a human top; a diver who leaped from an eighty-five-foot tower into a tank with three feet of water; and numerous other performers to catch the eye and turn the heads of every spectator.

Besides the action under the big top, many circuses provided sideshows where spectators—for a nominal price—could see oddities of nature, often labeled "freaks" in the nomenclature of the time. These acts included such treats and freaks as a "singing donkey;" a mesmerizing monkey who hypnotized other animals; a bearded lady, who in at least one case turned out to be a man much to the surprise of his female roommates; an "iron-jawed" woman; and a "talking horse." Among the human oddities, for instance, was Joe "the California Giant" Sullivan, who attracted many sideshow viewers with his towering seven-foot, five-inch height at a time when the average American man stood five feet, seven inches tall. Sullivan's arms hung three feet, nine inches in length, and his feet measured fifteen inches.

Sullivan, though, was shorter by an inch than "the Texas Giant," variously identified as Colonel Torvell or Colonel Powell in 1890s' newspapers in the Great Plains and Midwestern states where his circus toured. Torvell stood seven feet, eight inches tall. His sideshow fame ballooned after he married "the midget maiden" Henrietta Mority, who was a petite twenty-two inches tall, on August 9, 1892, in Missouri. The bride's mother, another circus employee, raised concerns about her daughter's nuptials and was only pacified after the manager elevated the newlyweds to the sideshow's featured attraction with their names in foot-high letters and granted substantial raises to the newlyweds. News accounts left unclear whether the new mother-in-law got a raise as well for withdrawing her complaints against the union.

While the heights of the giant and his petite bride were verifiable, many of the so-called sideshow oddities were phony, far from what they appeared to be. A seventh-grade Anthony, Kansas, boy in 1899 reported on his visit to the circus, noting, "I saw the three-legged boy when he did not have his three legs on." So, a lot of fakery was mixed in with the legitimate acts, leaving spectators to guess what was real and what was an illusion or a fraud.

"There's always fun in the circus," reported the *Walker Lake Bulletin* of Hawthorne, Nevada, in January 1893. "So, here's to the circus, with its sham and its tinsel; its city of dirty tents; its troupe of hard-working, travel-stained men and women; its animals from the elephants to the monkeys; and all that go to make it the greatest show on earth. May it always be as fruitful of as much happiness and instruction as it has been since the first days of the old cross-country exhibition. It is an American institution that we are all proud of."

In addition to the typical acrobatic, equestrian, and animal acts, some circuses included history lessons during the show. The 1893 Adam Forepaugh Circus during its matinee offered nine vignettes from the American Revolution, including Paul Revere's Ride, the battles of Concord Bridge and Bunker Hill, the signing of the Declaration of Independence, Washington crossing the Delaware, the surrender of Cornwallis, and the inauguration of George Washington as president, "all given in a very realistic manner to the great delight of the audience," according to the *Argus-Leader* of Sioux Falls.

Eureka, Nevada, hosted its first circus in 1877, then its second eleven months later in May 1878 when the *Daily Sentinel* noted, "The circus has come and gone; went away with quite a snug sum added to its exchequer, and left many pleasant memories behind it. After all, it is the popular amusement of the masses, the only one patronized alike by rich and poor, high and low, the place where the saint and sinner meet to mutually enjoy an entertainment that appeals with equal force to all classes and conditions. What other species of traveling aggregation could bring 5,000 people to its doors in a town that only boasts of 7,000 inhabitants?"

"The class of amusement, which is the most popular, is the circus, and the circuses of today are far in advance of any class of public entertainment," opined the *Dallas Daily Herald* in 1884. "The circus is popular because it is the amusement of the masses, and as circuses, like all things else, increase in popularity in accordance with the degree of merit possessed."

In South Dakota, the *Miller Press* implored readers to attend a June 1893 circus when it came to town. "Circus day will soon be here. Let your mind wander back to the days when the first rays of the sun found you up, ready to welcome the elephants into town. Take your little ones to the circus that exhibits here on Tuesday, June 27, and renew your childhood in contemplation of their delighted little faces. It is money well spent."

And spend their cash, they did. After an 1883 visit to Austin, the *American-Statesman* estimated the circus left town with $12,000, equaling almost $380,000 in 2025 purchasing power. The money may have been gone, but the memories lasted.

John Taylor Waldorf remembered his Virginia City circus experiences for decades. "As for the performance itself, some of us saw it and some of us didn't. I was invariably one of the favored. In eleven years beginning with the time when I saw Nellie Brown juggle knives while she rode two horses 'going at a maddening speed' until old John Robinson almost made me cross-eyed with his two rings, I missed just one circus. I shall always believe that one was the best circus that ever came west."

Waldorf missed that year because "fate had singled me out for punishment" for a misdeed, and he was forced to watch the "city of tents" from his backyard, bawling most of the time over his loss of privileges. "One of my sisters advised me to be careful lest my tears wash the fence away. Truly, it was the dampest day I ever spent."

Young Waldorf always regretted he had never carried water for the elephants, but felt glad he had never stuck his hand in a leopard's cage like one of his friends did, receiving a mauling in return. "Nine cats all clawing at once couldn't have given him the mark that he got from that leopard. His screams sound(ed) above the roar of the lion," Waldorf recalled. Waldorf did sneak under the tent once when a small road show called the Great Arabian Circus came to town. With only a single tent and no elephants, lions, or tigers, "it wasn't worth the trouble," Waldorf remembered.

The Decatur, Texas, newspaper in September 1889, observed, "Pity the small boy who has no money with which to buy a ticket. He will lie on his stomach for hours peeping under the crack at the bottom of the canvass, for the scanty gratification of seeing the legs of the performers, and listening to the sonorous crack of the whip as the ringmaster spurs up the horses and invigorates the riders with some of the stale jokes which is the stock in trade of the circus."

After an 1899 Ringling Brothers Circus visit to Anthony, Kansas, local school superintendent Theo Fulton assigned children in all grades to write essays about their experiences during the day and evening. He turned many of those papers over to the *Anthony Republican*, which printed some of the more interesting observations with this introduction: "Through the kindness of the superintendent we have been permitted to examine a number of the papers, and take pleasure in giving several of them in this number of the *Republican*. Our selection will probably not agree with the grades made by the teachers, as we have chosen from those we read, almost solely from the standpoint of interest to our readers and story value. The experience of the boy who worked his way into the circus, we are confident, will remind many of our readers of the past. "

In what the *Republican* called "a remarkable bit of work," a six-year-old wrote, "The circus was very nice, I thought. Did you? The wild animals were in cages. I thought the clowns were very funny. Did you? I thought the tumbling was very nice. I thought the horseback riders were nice. I saw a hippopotamus, too. When the elephants eat their dinner, I thought it was very funny. Did you?"

A third-grader wrote, "I have seen a number of shows, but I think the Ringling show is the best I ever saw. I watched them from early morning 'til late at night and saw them come to the show grounds with their large wagons drawn by eight horses. They seemed to raise their large and small tents with perfect ease. The horses, elephants, camels, and the holy cow walked from the train to the show grounds. The rest of the animals came in cages as you saw them in the parade. Then I watched them wash the bear and water the elephants."

Continuing, the third-grader noted, "The street parade was grand. I did not go to the sideshow or concert, so I cannot tell you anything about them. In the first large tent were the animals; there were elephants, camels, zebras, bears, lions, tigers, zebras, wolves, monkeys, Mexican hog, ostrich, parrots, and many others. In the next large tent was the circus. The best things I saw there were the trained elephants; the horse drill with the sixty-one horses; the three ladies and three gentlemen that did so many things; the trapeze actors; the lady riders; and the races. There was good music all the time. The clowns were funny. I liked the circus very much."

From a fourth-grader came this account: "In the big show, I saw an elephant stand on his head. I saw them lie down, and another elephant came into the ring and told him to get up, and he wouldn't do it; the police came in and hit him with a stick, and he hollered. I saw an elephant ring a bell for his supper, and then I seen two elephants sit up to the table and they sit on chairs and they would throw the dishes on the ground, and then his master would stick him with a sharp iron. And I saw them unload them from the cars."

An Anthony fifth-grader reported, "I attended Ringling Brothers circus Fri., Oct. 6, and enjoyed it very much; they had thirty-four cages of animals, and four cages of birds. The circus had twenty elephants. There are two kinds of elephants, the Indian and the African; the African elephant has large ears and large tusks, while the Indian elephant having small ears and no tusks. But about the elephants performing. There were six elephants in the ring. They would stand on their heads, lie down, sit on tubs and blow horns, when their master would tell them to."

The fifth-grader continued, "The American monkeys are found in South America, and are not usually found in North America. There were nineteen monkeys in one cage, two dogs, little rabbits, two little pigs, and one little kitty. The monkeys would hold out their little paws for popcorn, and if you would give them some, they would run off to a corner, eat it up, and come back and ask for more. The monkeys would try to perform in the little rings and swings that was in the cage. Monkeys are very amusing when you stand and look at them."

A sixth-grader observed, "Friday morning the streets were thronged with people to see the parade as it passed by. A very beautiful bandwagon led the procession, and a steam piano ended it. They had elephants in the parade and some cages, but only a few were open. It was a beautiful day, and the uniforms of the riders glittered in the sun. They had thirty-five trained horses and twenty-five trained elephants, which did many tricks. The little Japanese girl could bend backwards 'til her head touched the ground. There were four girls, which acted on horses and did it well. Two women and four men were tumblers. They were dressed just as other people, and they acted just as well or better than any of them. They had a good crowd, and I think all enjoyed it. I know I did."

A seventh-grade boy wrote, "At four o'clock in the morning of the Ringling Bros. show, I was standing down by the depot watching them unload. I saw them unload the horses and elephants and other animals. There was three trains come here. They had twenty elephants. Then we went down to the show grounds, and a man wanted us to work for a ticket to the show, and we unloaded two big wagon loads of trunks and then carried two buckets of water apiece about four blocks and then couldn't find the man we had been working for and went over to another place, and a man asked us if we wanted to work for a ticket to the show, and we said we had been working for the show all the morning, and he told us we had been working for the sideshow and that made us feel very cheap, so we worked for the big show and got our ticket.... The performing was very good."

An observant eighth-grader wrote about the arrival of the circus, the performing animals, and the patriotic performance on the Spanish-American War, which had ended the year before. Wrote the student, "It is wonderful how a great deal of work can be accomplished apparently so easily. Those who had the pleasure of witnessing the unloading of the Ringling Bros. circus were greatly surprised to see that there was no commotion, no profane language. The three trains were (un)loaded in less than two hours. It was very amusing to see the large animals come out of the cars; all but the larger elephants walked down on plank; the two largest elephants stepped from the car to the ground. Their horses were beautiful; they showed the best of care. It certainly required a great deal of patience as well as kindness to train these horses to perform as those in the circus. It shows how very intelligent a horse is. I think a horse comes next to man in intellect; they certainly have (an) ear for music; it looks like an impossibility for a horse to cakewalk, but Ringlings had one that could. A person would think an elephant was too large to be taught anything, but they can do a great many very funny things. It is strange how they can keep perfect time to music. Another thing is what perfect control the actors have of their nerves; for instance, during the high air performance, a part of one of the trapezes broke and came down; it must have been very heavy for it took about fifteen men to lift it. There were three actors on another part of the trapeze when it broke; they did not seem at all confused. The first act of the circus showed the managers were very patriotic. The centerpiece was Uncle Sam, the Goddess of Liberty, and Cuba in chains; these were removed by Uncle Sam."

A well-read tenth-grade girl familiar with William Allen White's *Kansas*—a series of short stories about boys growing up in Boyville, Kansas, and one, Bud Perkins, stealing a dollar from his mother's purse to attend the circus—wrote a poignant essay on the circus coming to town. "When I looked out in the morning and found the circus was on my side of town, I felt stuck up as did 'Bud Perkins' when the circus came to Boyville. I wished again, as I have wished so often, that I were a boy and could go and watch the process of unloading the animals. But, being 'only a girl,' I was obliged to wait for the parade. From a good position in an office, I watched and listened anxiously for the cry of the marshal, 'All horses off from Main Street!' For I knew the parade would soon appear. It came, at last, headed by a bandwagon gorgeous to behold, and the music was fine.

"The horses," she continued, "were beautiful and well managed. The elephants and camels, while they were as ugly as usual, were fine specimens. The bell-ringing was a novelty. The calliope played 'A Hot Time' in good style. Altogether, it presented a glittering spectacle. As for the circus, the animals were a natural-history lesson in themselves; most of them were fine, the ostrich, however, was a poor specimen. The horses were almost human in their sagacity. The training of the horse ridden by Madam Castello—and her management of it—was excellent. It is surprising to note what patience and endurance on the part of teacher and pupils as exemplified in training of the elephants and the docile obedience of those great brutes to the slightest word of command from their master. The trapeze and acrobatic performances were wonderful.

"I was impressed," she concluded, "by the systematic way in which everything was conducted, and I am not surprised that it takes five [Ringling] brothers to manage it. If the eight-thousand two hundred people carried away as pleasant impressions as I did, Ringling's circus will leave many pleasant memories behind it."

So spellbinding were all the wonders of the circus that youngsters would imitate what they saw for weeks after its departure or would run away to join the circus. Once the circus departed, it proved "to be epidemic, and some boys are badly affected," reported the 1880 *Canton Advocate* in Dakota Territory. "The advent of a circus is all that is needed to drive them stark, staring mad, and bring forth extraordinary and superhuman gymnastic exercises. The past experience of Canton boys would seem to point to the fact that 'playing circus' is a dangerous pastime; but they keep right along, leaping, tumbling, twisting, and risking their precious necks."

From the Great Plains to the Pacific, boys and girls as young as ten left home for the big top. In 1890s Nebraska, Flora Hines, seventeen, abandoned her Lincoln home for the circus, as did young Ned Stoughton of Falls City. In Beatrice, George Howe, Marion Hawkins, and Willie Werner, all thirteen, escaped home to join the circus in Lincoln. Seventeen-year-old Anna Schremp departed Hartington to hook up with a circus in Iowa. Five Blair girls, ages ten to fifteen, answered the siren call of the circus and ran away from home. On the Pacific Coast in California, Otis Day of Lorin, Joe Pratt of Visalia, Guy Silcox of San Jose, and Frank Kelly of Calistoga all abandoned home for the circus life. From Denison, Texas, Harry Alsop, Tom Sparr, Will May, Jack Starr, and Harry Beamer, ranging in age from fourteen to eighteen, forsook their parents to join the circus in Kansas City and "to see the world." The Texas quintet got only as far as Guthrie, Oklahoma, before authorities detained them and sent them home. Like the Texas five, most runaways returned home, either of their own volition or with the help of police.

The story of two Arkansas siblings in 1881 illustrates the draw of the circus. The seventeen-year-old girl and her fifteen-year-old brother had traveled with their parents named Wallace more than a hundred miles to see the circus in Little Rock. The sister and brother decided they would join the circus without telling their parents and slipped away from them, the girl donning shabby boy clothes so her gender wouldn't hinder her plans. Both hired on for two dollars a week and from Little Rock traveled through the greater part of Texas, "the glitter and tinsel of the business fading away at every stop," according to the Little Rock newspaper.

Circus management fired the pair in Galveston, leaving them stranded more than five hundred miles from their Arkansas home with only five dollars to their names. With their childish ingenuity and the charity of sympathizers, the pair eventually made it back to Searcy, Arkansas, and their relieved parents, much wiser than when they abandoned their folks for the circus.

The *Woman's Exponent* of Salt Lake City, wrote of the problem in 1872. "There have been several instances lately out West of girls who have run away to join the circus. What a joy it must be to a gentle maiden to array herself in gauze and spangles, and dash through paper-covered hoops, and associate with teamsters and rowdyish circus men."

Assessing the problem, the *Brookings Register* in 1898 South Dakota wrote, "Many a boy who runs away to join a circus is only too glad to walk back home again." In Kansas, the *Mound Valley Herald* summed up the problem by a supposed conversation between two young boys: "First boy (in surprise)—'Why, I heard you ran off to join a circus. Didn't you catch it?' Second boy—'Not 'til I got back home'."

Circus runaways were such a common experience that even theatrical plays were written about them, including *Circus Queen*, which toured western theaters during the 1890s about a young woman who joins the circus to escape her abusive father. Though nowhere near as flamboyant as the circus, theatrical performances provided another form of frontier entertainment and escape for children.

Virginia City youth John Taylor Waldorf, who would get up at two o'clock in the morning to see the circus train arrive, decided he wanted to become an actor after watching his first theatrical performance. His dream of stage acting was fraught "with fond hopes and bitter disappointment," though he occasionally risked life and limb just to see a play. When a low-budget theatrical troupe visited Virginia City and sought local boys to perform as soldiers in colorful red, yellow, and blue Zouave uniforms, Waldorf applied. The stage manager dismissed him with, as Waldorf recalled later, words of doom: "You won't do, kid. You're too small."

Vowing revenge on the stage manager, he slipped in an unlocked side door the next afternoon and watched the performance without paying, even though the sheriff had seen him and eight other boys slide through the unlocked door. Another time, Waldorf and a friend, both without enough money to afford a ticket, found a ladder, propped it up against the wall and climbed up onto the theater roof. They scurried along the rooftop to a skylight that they loosened and lifted so they could slip into the garret. They stepped from rafter to rafter until they seated themselves "on a great beam at least ten feet above the lofty perch occupied by the curtain-raisers." From there they watched the production below of *Macbeth*, the only disadvantage being that if they slipped, they'd fall sixty feet into the cheap two-dollar seats.

"If you never saw a play from above the stage, you can't appreciate its advantages," Waldorf remembered. "We watched the actors loafing between the flies, saw them dashing off the stage, and then stopping as suddenly as if someone had yanked them with a lariat. But that wasn't all. Even the 'bully' duel wasn't the best thing. We saw dead men get up and walk (afterward)." Noted his gatecrashing friend, "That's more'n we'd get if we'd paid two dollars."

Not just boys were enthralled with the theater. At the age of eleven, Willa Cather in 1885 attended her first theatrical performance in the Red Cloud Opera House on the Nebraska town's main street. The auditorium, seating five hundred, was built on the second floor above a local hardware store and was lighted by reflector kerosene lamps.

"To be sure, the opera house was dark for most of the year, but that made its events only the more exciting. Half a dozen times during each winter—in the larger towns much oftener—a traveling stock company settled down at the local hotel and thrilled and entertained us for a week. That was a wonderful week for children," Cather recalled in 1929 for the *Omaha World-Herald*.

The excitement began with the advance men, who— just like circus promoters—plastered the town with flyers and placards on barns and fences and in the windows of drug stores and grocery stores. A traveling troupe might spend a week in a town and perform a different play every night to sell as many tickets as possible and keep the auditorium full.

"My playmates and I used to stand for an hour after school, studying every word on those posters; the names of the plays and the nights on which each would be given. After we had decided which were the most necessary to us, then there was always the question of how far we could prevail upon our parents. Would they let us go every other night, or only the opening and closing nights? None of us ever got to go every night, unless we had a father who owned stock in the opera house itself."

Learning when the theater troupe would arrive, Cather and her girlfriends walked a half mile to the train depot to await the appearance of the stars and share in the glamor of their occupation. "We found it delightful," she recalled, "to watch the theatrical company alight, pace the platform while their baggage was being sorted, and then drive off— the men in the hotel bus, the women in the 'hack.' If by chance one of the show ladies carried a little dog with a blanket on, that simply doubled our pleasure."

Cather recalled the Andrews Opera Company with "a good voice or two among them, a small orchestra and a painstaking conductor, who was also the pianist," performing *The Bohemian Girl*, *The Chimes of Normandy* and *Martha* and others. "What good luck for a country child to hear those tuneful old operas sung by people who were doing their best," she recalled. Other theatrical companies put on plays like *My Partner*, *The Corsican Brothers*, *Ingomar*, *Damon and Pythias*, and *The Count of Monte Cristo*.

Though Cather and Waldorf were enthralled with the theater, neither ever acted on stage. James Carden did. In 1851, in the wake of the California Gold Rush, Carden made his first theatrical appearance, playing "Gaspard" in *Lady of Lyons* before an audience of appreciative Forty-niners in Nevada City, California. He was twelve years old at the time and soon performed in nearby Grass Valley, California, as "Wilford" in the *Iron Chest*. Becoming the pet of the mining camps, Carden decided to make a career of greasepaint and limelight, eventually appearing on stage in New York and later in Australia and England, where he married eminent actress Marston Leigh. They ultimately settled in San Francisco, and in 1885, thirty-four years after his Nevada City debut, he returned to the community for an encore for a career well played.

William J. Cartin, thirteen, of St. Louis was another stage-struck youth after seeing *Richard III* in his hometown theater. He soon learned the play and trained his own dramatic company of playmates to stage plays in costumes he secured and on a stage built in his father's backyard. Such tenacity and dedication to the theatrical arts soon earned him minor roles in a theater company's repertoire.

Though not as flamboyant as circuses, theatrical performances also provided eye-opening entertainment for pintsized pioneers. The two venues also helped provide an outlet for spreading the myth of the American West around the globe and preserving it for posterity. William F. "Buffalo Bill" Cody, who became the world's preeminent purveyor of the frontier mythology, patterned his Wild West show after the circus, both in performance and in logistics.

His stage experience also helped him understand the value of showmanship and keeping an audience. Circuses taught Cody the power of grand visuals with extravagant pageantry, bold costumes, flags, music, and action-packed acts, replacing elephants with buffalo and acrobats with Native Americans. He patterned his advance men after the circus and theatrical models with ostentatious posters and attention-grabbing parades to drum up interest and business. He adapted circus logistics to his Wild West needs, traveling by rail with customized rail cars for animals, performers, props, and equipment.

Ultimately, Buffalo Bill Cody took the circus format, stripped away the trapeze and wild animals, replacing them with cowboys, cavalry, and Indians. In doing so, he developed an entertainment form that blended frontier nostalgia, showmanship, theatrical staging, and patriotic spectacle into what he marketed as "a national history lesson." After the turn of the century, Buffalo Bill's performances with their circus and theatrical influences helped shape the nation's emerging movie industry by making the Western a staple of early filmmaking.

Chapter Seven

Books and Bibles

Twenty-first century youngsters might have a hard time identifying school as play, but for frontier children, particularly ones living in rural areas on homesteads and isolated ranches, school offered a break from their chores and a chance to visit and frolic with others their age. Even so, the classroom regimentation necessary to provide a satisfactory learning environment annoyed the more free-spirited among the students leading some, usually boys though not always, to skip school and play hooky.

While school offered lessons for their intellectual development, another frontier institution—the church, regardless of the various denominations—provided moral instruction for the youngsters' spiritual growth in a challenging environment where laws and their enforcement were often sparse. In the early years on the frontier or in newly settled regions later, school and church lessons were frequently taught by the children's mother at home where chores always took precedence.

Years after her eastern New Mexico Territory childhood, Lily Klasner recalled, "I can still hear Mother call after supper. 'Come, children, get your books and study your lessons.' That was after we had fed the chickens and cooped each brood it its home; had fed the hogs; had carried the night's supply of water, cobs, wood, and chips; had helped with the evening meal and the dishwashing; had washed crocks in which the milk was strained; and had put the younger children to bed. Then we studied."

In families where the mother was literate, she taught her offspring the alphabet and numbers, then turned to spelling, rudimentary grammar, and arithmetic. With reading materials scarce on the early frontier, the only book might be the family Bible, which served as a reader, a storybook, and a moral guidebook.

As printing technology advanced after the Civil War, books became more affordable, and families could buy *Webster's Blue-Backed Speller*, a crucial guide for spelling instruction on the frontier; and *McGuffey Readers*, a series of six primers for first through sixth grades. The readers offered moral lessons, often with patriotic and religious themes, while teaching reading, spelling, and vocabulary. The first volumes taught vocabulary and reading through basic phonics, while the later readers grew more complex with instruction in classic literature and oratory.

Sometimes rural neighbors banded together for their children's education and pooled their resources to hire a teacher. Eleanor Mitchell Traweek wrote of such an arrangement in the 1890s Texas Panhandle. "It was not uncommon for a family whose ranch was inaccessible to a school to hire a governess to live in their home to teach their children. Maggie Hamilton acted as a governess for the A.B. Echols ranch, and taught both the Echols children and the Johnny Miller children who lived at Miller's Springs. Lena Miller and her big brother Fred left little sister Dollie at home, and rode over by horseback every morning to go to the ranch 'school' with Beulah and Bob

Echols.... The children studied readin' and 'ritin' and 'rithmetic and, in addition, English, spelling, and geography."

In other areas, neighbors banded together to build a primitive schoolhouse with few amenities. Looking back at her pioneer education on the barren plains, Vera Pearson remembered the stark simplicity of those early schoolhouses. "They had a few bare benches, flat, without backs, and so far off the floor that little legs, dangling high in the air, would ache cruelly before a change of position was possible. An extra-brave or desperate pupil might lie down a bit to relieve the strain, but the season of relief would be short-lived. No charts, no maps, no pictures, no books but a speller. They would have 'numbers' later but some of the little fellows never got that far."

A student identified only as "Jim," who attended school in the late 1880s in the Montana mining country, said, "I went to school out on Basin Creek, a one-room school with everything from the first grade to the eighth grade. It would vary, but anywhere from, I'd say, ten to probably at the highest wouldn't have been over fifteen students." Besides student shortages, rural schools also lacked teaching supplies.

John Kooken, a Texas student who became a teacher, recalled the primitive conditions in the 1880s classroom. "The furniture consisted of long benches made without adjustment to pupils from seven to twenty years of age. Twelve-inch boards were attached to the long benches by means of strap hinges. During the writing periods, the boards were raised on the hinges and a prop-stick extending from the floor was used to hold the board in position for writing. The equipment consisted of a very limited supply of blackboard, which was constructed of three pieces of one-by-twelve, framed and painted black. When the school opened on that October morning, the children, their dogs and about half of the patrons (parents) were present. The children brought in every variety of readers, spellers, and arithmetics; a dinner bucket with large biscuits, smokehouse cured ham, and a wide-mouthed quinine bottle filled with homemade molasses, and a bottle of milk.... The children and the dogs belonging to the family gathered around the dinner bucket. Each child took one of those large biscuits, bored a hole in the middle of the top crust with his forefinger and filled the hole with homemade molasses from the above mentioned quinine bottle [for lunch]."

Dotty Jones remembered the 1880s Texas Panhandle town of Farwell's country school. "The children carried their lunches in lard buckets. They usually took bread, butter, and jelly, or bacon or beef sandwiches, or fried chicken. They either walked or rode horseback, or rode in a horse- or donkey-drawn cart. If a child had a disease, such as measles or whooping cough, the child continued to attend school, and everyone usually had the disease before it was over."

Early schools faced other challenges. M.M. Kennedy recalled a primitive 1830s Texas class. "The school was in summertime, and during the long, hot days, the wild cattle came to the grove around the schoolhouse to stamp in the shade. Their bellowing and fighting often monopolized our attention to the annoyance of the teacher, and often [presented] serious danger to our horses. 'Tis an ill wind that blows nobody good.' It was necessary to drive these cattle away, which was by no means the simple thing it is to drive gentle cattle. We [boys] had to go in force, and when the enemy was routed, we were apt to become dispersed in pursuit, and it took time to rally."

Despite their schools' many deficiencies and challenges, some children remembered them as noble institutions, the seedbed of frontier civilization. James

Rooney reminisced years later about the White House School in Fort Stockton, Texas, as it was in 1879: "It seemed, as I recall it, a lonely little house of scholarship, with its playground worn so bare that even the months of sun and idleness failed to bring forth any grass. But that humble little school had a dignity of a fixed and far-off purpose. It was the nest of the West's greatness. It was the outpost of civilization. It was the advance guard of the pioneer, driving the wilderness farther into the West. It was life preparing wistfully for the future. The school was poorly equipped, indeed, since it boasted only a few long, crude benches, with no desks but the knees upon which to write."

To address the shortfall of books and supplies, students brought from home what resources they had, whether books of Mother Goose nursery rhymes, outdated almanacs, magazines, and even newspapers. With limited materials, the emphasis started on reading, writing, spelling, grammar, and basic arithmetic. The curriculum expanded to geography, history, and even geometry when suitable books and maps could be obtained. Generally, all the grades—from first through sixth or even eighth—were taught in the same classroom, complicating the teacher's job. As Vera Pearson stated, "The miracle was that a love of 'learning' ever survived the rigors of school days then. But it did in some cases."

Martha Hutchison, looking back on her education, said, "I was twelve years old, and there were not many advantages for a child of that age in a new country where there were no schools, no papers, no books, and whose parents could neither read nor write." Roxana Rice remembered the first school she attended on the plains as "a room crowded full of big boys and girls, noise and confusion with now and then a howl from some boy that was being whipped. I and my brother with another boy occupied a bench with no back near the stove. When the stove became too warm, we whirled and faced the other side. The boy with us wore a paddle fastened around his neck. On this paddle were pasted several letters of the alphabet, and these were changed every day. How I envied that boy because his folks were making so much pains with him. The attention given him I coveted, though the letters he paraded I knew as well as I do today."

Early on the frontier, men dominated the impromptu teaching corps. Only after the Civil War did women outnumber men in the Old West classroom. Male teachers had the advantage of keeping order in the rough-and-tumble spirit of the early classroom, while females brought a more civilizing touch, making the classroom as cozy an environment as possible. The men paddled the truants while the women papered the walls with pages ripped from magazines and newspapers, with student drawings and with hand-lettered adages like "Honesty is the best policy," "Look before you leap," and "Knowledge is Power."

Teaching methods and classroom exercises were often odd. One western teacher was a deserter from the British Navy who during cold weather "warmed his scholars by having them join hands and run around whilst he hastened their speed by the free use of a stick." Another male instructor in Texas used what he termed as "the loud method" to teach reading. When students read aloud at the same time, he ordered them to shout at the top of their voices to drown each other out. Whether or not "the loud method" was effective remains undocumented, but passing travelers commented about the lessons being heard a considerable distance from the schoolhouse.

Discipline was a problem. In the early years on the Arkansas frontier, a male teacher named Anderson tried to stop two Madden brothers from bullying other students. When they were slow responding, he jerked them from the melee they had created and gave them both a solid paddling, then sent them home. When the siblings reached their cabin and told their father of the teacher's abuse, the old man stormed to the school and demanded to know why his boys—but not the others involved in the dispute—had been whipped.

Anderson explained to the father that his sons had instigated the difficulties and that "the others were fighting in self-defense." Dissatisfied with the answer, the dad said he would whip the teacher after class. The elder Madden remained on the school grounds until the last class ended. The two men then exchanged blows, punching and wrestling each other until they were bloodied, bruised, and exhausted. Observers finally broke up the fight, calling it a draw.

The pugilists went their separate ways, and when the father arrived back at the Madden cabin, his wife asked if he was going to allow their sons to go back to school as long as Anderson remained the schoolmaster. Replied the father, "Dag-goon, yes. Any man that can whip my boys, then beat me up can teach my kids."

In New Mexico, one nineteenth-century teacher carried a pistol under his coat for protection against his students, though the weapon was of little use when one boy slipped up behind him with a logging chain and knocked him unconscious.

Women teachers, by contrast, may not have brought iron fists to the classroom, but they did offer a gentler, more civilized touch, like the young female teacher in Washington Territory during the Civil War. She had traveled from another state to teach and insisted that the school board provide an outhouse. One critic griped that this was what happened when they hired someone from outside the territory. "Never had any trouble before, plenty of trees to get behind," the detractor wailed. After the young teacher threatened to quit, the board gave in and approved the outdoor toilet.

Young teacher Lydia Murphy was another perceived troublemaker in Johnson County, Kansas, when she decided to teach geography and was challenged by a male board member for even thinking of teaching "joggerphy," as he called it. Complained the board member, "Miss Murphy, it wouldn't be so bad if it was just boys, but we think too much of the girls to have them spoiled, their religion taken away by teaching joggerphy." With a little persuasion and the singing of a song used to help children remember the capitals of each state, Miss Murphy convinced the skeptic otherwise. As she remembered the difficulty years later, "From that time on I taught geography without interruption, and no apparent corruption of morals or religion ensued."

Western lecturer Josh Billings described the typical frontier schoolmarm. "She is the paragon of propriety and had rather be three years behind in styles than to spell one word wrong or to parse a sentence incorrectly.... She is stepmother to more bad boys children than anybody else and has the patience and forbearance of Job with naughty boys and stupid girls.... She works the hardest and gets the nearest to no pay for it of any person I know in a civilized and Christian land."

In Cook County, Texas, young Melissa Everett was so excited when a newly arrived preacher agreed to teach local classes. "My father told me how he wanted me to go every day, and I wanted an education so bad." Her formal education lasted but ten days when a death in the preacher/teacher's family called him away for good. "Now," she recalled years later, "I have pulled through this long life in ignorance." Everett underestimated her intellect because she had educated herself enough to be able to read, write, and speak with an understated elegance.

Such was education on the frontier; children had to make the best of what the circumstances presented them.

Self-education was as important as formal education. Arizona siblings J.W. LaSeur and his brother hungered to read so much that they would stand on their heads to peruse the newspapers pasted upside-down on the walls of their family's cabin.

By the 1880s, books, made affordable by the mass publishing from improved printing technology, could be purchased through mail-order catalogs. Dime novels became available, and little boys—and even young girls— thrilled at the adventures of such print heroes as Moccasin Mose, Squint-Eyed Bob, and Old Neversleep. In Colorado, Ann Ellis read everything she could, from dime novels to Plutarch's *Lives* and from Dumas to Zola. "The greatest influence in my life has been books, good books, bad books, and indifferent ones," Ellis remembered later.

As an adult, John Taylor Waldorf said he "would turn up my nose and look insulted" if someone offered him a dime novel to read, but his reading tastes were different as a child. "When I was a boy in Virginia City, the sixteen-page and thirty-two-page pamphlet-like novels with a thrill or two on every page, and just the size to hide behind an open geography book, gave me countless hours of delight. It wasn't only in the reading that I found pleasure but in the hope of someday becoming a detective greater than Old Neversleep or an Indian fighter braver than Moccasin Mose."

Continued Waldorf, "Lest anyone think that my ambition was narrow, I here record a confession that I wanted to be at least nine kinds of hero. I stood ready, or thought I did, to trail thieves, stop runaways, put down a mutiny on shipboard, rescue beautiful maidens from burning buildings, lead the palefaces against bloodthirsty redskins—in fact, do any and everything that might possibly make haughty folk say in admiring tones as I passed by, 'There goes the boy hero'."

Unlike their frontier peers, children on army posts had easier access to schooling after 1866 when Congress authorized teaching facilities at garrisons, though the procedures varied from fort to fort. In 1881's revised *Army Regulations*, the military formalized school practices, setting morning class hours from 9:30 a.m. until noon and afternoon sessions from 1-3 p.m. The classes were also open to illiterate soldiers when their schedules permitted. Some soldiers even taught courses, receiving an additional thirty-five cents a day in extra-duty pay. Children from the surrounding communities could attend, if their folks made a modest contribution to the post's schooling fund. Soldiers and citizens alike provided books and supplies the youngsters used for their lessons.

The teaching varied from post to post. Attending classes in the 1870s at Fort Laramie, Jake Tomamichel remembered one soldier who taught the regular subjects, but during recess also instructed his students on how to become detectives. Recess turned out to be young Jake's favorite lesson. At Fort McKinney in 1889, Guy Henry, Jr., recalled the principal teachers were two deserters who taught class with "heavy iron shackles around their ankles." Educational quality varied as young Guy learned when he returned with his officer father and mother to Danville, New York, where they enrolled him in the local school. After testing him, school officials put him in the first grade even though he was much older than the typical first-grader. Noted Guy, "I knew little about reading, spelling, and arithmetic, while I was well-versed in lightning, thunder, vapor (clouds), and geography."

Under the army rules, teachers could not administer corporal punishment, though they could send misbehaving students to stand in the corner or wear the dunce cap for a while.   Those regulations prohibited enlisted men's children from being expelled, though they were to be "corrected from time to time until good behavior resulted." The children of officers who misbehaved could be suspended from class or, if unacceptable behavior persisted, expelled from school.   One such student was Dick Dana.

Reverend Alexander Gilmore served as the post chaplain at Whipple Barracks, Arizona Territory, and also taught school in nearby Prescott, where young Dana, the son of an army major, was a persistent troublemaker. Accused—falsely according to him—of targeting a classmate "over the head with a spit gob," Dana accepted his punishment and stood "behind the master's chair wearing the fool's cap." Noticing the schoolmaster's wig was slipping as he nodded at recitations, Dana yanked the toupee from his teacher's noggin, ran outside, and mounted his horse.   He galloped off, waving the hairpiece and screaming, "I've got ole Gilmore's scalp, and here it is!" Dana was dismissed from school for that prank, drawing the disappointment of a fellow student who noted, "We don't have no more fun now since Dick Dana was expelled."

Just getting to class could be a challenge on the frontier.   M.M. Kennedy remembered an 1835 school in Austin's Colony while Mexico still ruled Texas. His eight-year-old elder brother attended the school, which was "about two miles from our house, and the way was through woods without any road or path.   When he started to school, our father was absent, and mother went with him, carrying a hatchet to blaze the way."

A young girl identified only as "Catherine" in the Butte, Montana, mining community remembered the winters and the trek to class with more than fifty classmates. "We had to cross the railroad track from our house to St. Mary's School. And believe me, it was snow. It was knee-deep getting back and forth to that school." The frigid discomfort continued even after they reached the classroom. Remembered Catherine, "It was cold, and if you'd sit over by the window, and there was a big blizzard, well, the snow all came in the window, 'cause it was poorly built, just haphazardly built. They had a boiler—when it worked. At one time, they used coal. They used all kinds of coal. Then the Anaconda Company got generous, and they piped in steam from the Steward Mine into St. Mary's School. But that didn't warm it any. You still sat with your overshoes and sweaters and coats on during school hours."

Weather affected not only the comfort of the students but their attendance. Whether hot or cold, youngsters found a reason to cut school and play hooky. "The average small boy about town," observed the *Kingman Journal* during a frigid Kansas January, "has been playing 'hooky' since skating has been good." During an especially cold winter start in November 1880 in Lawrence, the *Kansas Daily Tribune* opined, "If the present weather continues, the price of skates will advance, and the youth will return to his parents from playing 'hooky' with a lump back of his ear, caused by the attraction of gravity." A March *Horton Commercial* blurb in Kansas noted the approach of spring. "This warm weather is too much for the schoolboys. They have commenced playing 'hooky'." By May, the *Osborne County Farmer*, also in Kansas, was reporting, "School is out, and now the small boys can go swimming and fishing without playing 'hooky'."

Particularly in western towns and cities, newspapers viewed hooky as a problem, and local authorities responded. In 1876 San Jose, California, the *Mercury* reported, "The appointment of an officer to look after our truants is working admirably. Many a boy has found to his sorrow that playing 'hooky' is a bad business. Parents have been surprised, in several instances to learn that their boys, whom they supposed were attending school regularly, had not been inside of a schoolroom for weeks."

Nevada's *Yerington Times* in May 1875 observed, "It seems to us that the school law is not being very rigidly enforced in this vicinity. We see many children playing in the streets who should be in school. We counted ten urchins peering into the door of one saloon yesterday."

The *McPherson Daily Republican* of Kansas in the fall of 1890 reported on another way of stopping hooky. "There was weeping and wailing and gnashing of teeth among the boys of the city last night. A great number have been playing hooky from school, and it had come to such a pass that the fathers could stand it no longer, and last night the matter was settled in the old-fashioned way. It is said they ran a regular tan yard for a while, or at least the boys thought so. We will venture to say that there were none absent from school today." Nine years later in Fredonia, Kansas, the *Wilson County Citizen* used the term "blue spots" as a synonym for "bruises." Reported the paper, "Blue spots, if worn in the right place, will cure boys from playing 'hooky' and prevent them from going out of town and boring into farmers' maple trees." The Sedgwick, Kansas, *Pantagraph*, wrote in 1893, "Kids on the streets at all hours of the day and night are a nuisance, especially when there is a school in session where they should be preparing themselves for the stern battles of life instead of hanging around on the street corners learning all kinds of devilment."

While boys were the most frequent hooky participants, girls also skipped school occasionally. The *Daily Bee* in 1888 Oswego, Kansas, reported, "Eight scared looking, sweet-faced schoolgirls made their appearance at the door of *The Bee* sanctum this afternoon, and lo, and behold, upon close inquiry, we learned they were playing 'hooky.' It isn't our impression they came here for the purpose of getting a personal [ad], nor do we intend to say a word about them having been here, but, girls, you shouldn't play 'hooky'." The *McPherson Daily Republican* of Kansas, seven years later observed and warned, "Cupid is responsible for one of the schoolgirls playing hooky to have an opportunity to chat with her beau in a corner of a store. Better look out. Cupid contracts debts, which he does not intend to pay."

To counter truancy and other impediments to student education, some school boards, like Woodville Academy in Tyler County, Texas, adopted rules for pupils to follow. The second rule in Woodville's list of fourteen was "students on leaving home must proceed without delay or loitering at any public place, directly to school and when dismissed in the evening retire in the same manner to their respective home." Inside the classroom, the rules prohibited "cursing, lying, swearing, stealing, wrestling, boxing, fighting, quarreling, nicknaming, backbiting or mischievous tale-bearing, or any other unbecoming language." Furthermore, the rules forbade "talking and whispering … unless about lessons." Outside the schoolroom, late-night activities "and other night rambles," including dances "or other kindred amusements," were forbidden on school nights unless written permission from the parent or guardian was presented to the teacher. Further, the rules stated, "In no event is the Sabbath to be broken by students."

The rule about observing the Sabbath tried to instill values in the students, but some moral lessons on the frontier could be stark as in the case of the Diamond City, Montana, teacher who took his class to see the dangling corpse of an overnight lynching victim to illustrate the wages of sin. The overlap of school and church was common as some communities used the same building for both. For instance, in 1870 near Wilmington, Kansas, an abandoned cabin on the inactive Santa Fe Trail served as the local schoolhouse and a place of worship on Sundays and religious holidays.

Just as early frontier schooling occurred in the settlers' primitive homes, so too were initial church services. Sometimes, they we just family devotionals, but with time neighbors—sometimes coming from miles away—would gather in a home for worship. Those occasions were not only a devotional experience, but also a social gathering that allowed distant neighbors to visit and dine together. And, their children could play with each other.

Lydia Murphy recalled how her parents, devout Methodists, in 1860 in Monticello Township, twenty miles west of Kansas City, secured a Methodist minister to conduct regular religious rites and then invited neighbors of differing faiths, Baptists, Unitarians, Episcopalians, and others to attend. "Arrangements were made for services every two weeks at our house. Saturday afternoon and evening was the day selected.... Sister Ella was given the duty of keeping the babies as quiet as possible upstairs. Brother Emmett entertained the young children with games in the yard, while the older children and I were allowed to be a part of the meeting. What fervent 'amens' arose during the sermon! The walls fairly shook with the Methodist hymns.... For years the meetings were held in our home, later being changed to Sunday.... These meetings were social as well as religious and provided a needed break from the hard toil of the empire-building, homemaking pioneers, except an occasional quilting, sheep-shearing or sorghum-making gathering."

The socializing usually included a great meal of sliced hams and fried chicken in the summer and beef or pork roasts in the winter, according to one Kansas girl, who recalled the delicious cream layer cakes "with the rich gooey mixture between layers," or the marble cakes spiced with cloves, cinnamon, and allspice. The Kansas lass continued, "That wasn't enough, though—the cookie jar must be kept well filled. There were the white cookies, which fairly melted in your mouth. The gingersnaps to eat with milk or coffee or maybe a soft gingerbread. I can taste that gingerbread yet. Truly a dish for the gods. Pies, of course, dried peach or apple or green tomato, or if she wished a one-crust pie there were vinegar, cream, custard, or pumpkin. If the dried fruit were used, it was first soaked overnight, then stewed and sweetened. If you never ate one, you don't know what you've missed."

Because ordained ministers were scarce, some denominations, like Baptists and Methodists, established circuit-riding preachers, who tended to a flock spread over dozens of square miles. They served the religious needs of adults and children throughout the region and relied on the tithe of those worshippers to support their own families. Since money was always tight on prairie homesteads, the circuit rider's worshippers gave what they could. The minister might return to his home with meat, chickens, eggs, flour, cornmeal, sorghum molasses, and anything else his parishioners could spare.

May Woodburn, daughter of Reverend John Woodburn, a Methodist minister who served the 1860s Nemaha County, Kansas, circuit, first on horseback and later in a springboard wagon, remembered, "He would leave home usually on a Saturday and be gone, sometimes for several days. During these absences from home, he would visit at the homes of his parishioners, and when he returned, he would bring with him the donations, which he had received. I well remember how we children waited to see what Father would bring home."

She continued, "In those days, money was very scarce, and the itinerant preacher received very little of it indeed. Father would bring home such things as potatoes, turnips, onions, meat, chickens, sacks of cornmeal and sometimes even discarded clothing and old toys. I remember some dolls, which were sent us children. They were old and worn, but they were the only ones we had and very dear to us.... We children were sometimes critical of the things he brought, especially the clothing. Some of it, we thought, was not good enough to be made over, and we wanted to use it for dressing up in our play. But this, Mother would never allow. She always preserved a sweet spirit about the donations. She insisted that the things we received were gifts and should be taken thankfully and never spoken of with levity."

But even the generosity of his parishioners could not support Reverend Woodburn's eleven children, and he also worked as a carpenter and stonemason to make ends meet.

As churches became more numerous on the Great Plains, services moved from the homes or schoolhouses to town and became more impersonal. Misbehavior, especially among boys but sometimes among girls as well, became enough of an issue for various newspapers to report on the misconduct. Kansas papers were especially observant of church behavior. In Altoona, the *Advocate* in 1886 headed a column "What the *Advocate* would Like to See" and listed, among other things, "more people come in and subscribe for the *Advocate*" and "less racket from the boys when church lets out." In 1899 Oskaloosa, the *Independent* reported, "We have been called upon several times to mention the misbehavior of some boys in church, but we notice that there are a few young ladies in town that need to be called down as bad as some of the boys."

The problem was serious enough in 1888 Osawatomie that the *Graphic* suggested turning the miscreants over to the authorities. "Several boys at church last Sunday night conducted themselves in a manner that strong talk was had in regard to arresting them. Boys, or even girls, that cannot attend church and observe a proper degree of decorum, should be promptly arrested and fined. The church is no place to go and indulge in frivolities, and the sooner the young folks find this out, the better it will be for them in the future." The *Barton County Democrat* in Great Bend, Kansas, observed, "Bad boys at church annoy other people and do discredit to themselves."

Occasionally the unruly behavior got out of hand, like in Butler Church near Star City, Arkansas, in 1897, when Thad Butler and Jesse Person, both fourteen, brawled during the religious service. Reported the papers, "Both boys used their knives and fought viciously. Butler was cut five times and Person was stabbed near the heart. Both boys will die. The fight occurred while the minister was delivering his sermon, and the congregation left the church in much confusion."

But childhood behavior had a benevolent side as well. In 1896 Santa Barbara, California, the Boys and Girls Brigade of Grace Methodist Church pledged during the Easter Service to contribute earnings to the benevolence fund. Each boy and girl was given a dime to invest, and two months later they returned with their profits. The boys raised $10.50 while the girls produced $17.50.

Frontier church sermons offered a powerful blend of the Scriptures, moral exhortation, and fire-and-brimstone warnings intended to save folks from eternal damnation. Such sermons resonated enough with one group of Kansas children that they made up a game called "Heaven and Hell," with a haystack serving as heaven and a cellar providing the nether reaches of hell. Two boys played God and Gabriel and another boy presided over the cellar as the devil, while the other children were sinners facing the Judgment Day. The pintsized God and Gabriel determined who went where among the sinners, and one account said, "Since each [sinner] was anxious to experience what hell was like, there were more fit subjects for hell than heaven."

The unifying element among school, church, and home was the Bible, often the only book in a frontier household. The Bible was not only a sacred text but also an educational resource. Children and even some adults learned to read by sounding out verses, memorizing Psalms, and practicing penmanship by copying passages on paper or slate. In one-room schoolhouses, the Bible served as a source for morning readings or recitations, particularly when no formal textbooks were available.

Additionally, the Bible offered the primary source of moral guidance with parents, educators, and preachers using biblical parables to instill the values of honesty, hard work, obedience, justice, and perseverance in children. The story of David and Goliath taught courage and faith in God, even when faced with overwhelming odds. That was an important lesson on the frontier, where struggles against nature, economic hardship, and enemies provided regular challenges. The parable of the Good Samaritan reflected compassion, charity, and helping neighbors, even strangers, all virtues essential to survival on the frontier. Mutual assistance could be the difference between life and death. The story of Joseph and his brothers emphasized faith and patience in suffering and showed the healing power of forgiveness. The Ten Commandments provided moral guideposts for life with moral expectations based on respect for God, parents, and neighbors, for honesty and faithfulness and for the sanctity of life. The Book of Proverbs provided concise adages for a successful life.

Stories like those impressed six brothers growing up in the onetime cattle town of Abilene, Kansas, in the late nineteenth century. Bible reading and prayer were a regular practice in their home and at the local Brethren in Christ Church, where the brothers attended Sunday School and religious services. The third of those brothers—Dwight David Eisenhower—would grow up to become the nation's Thirty-fourth President. Those values, learned at home, in school, in church, and later at West Point, would influence the course of his military and political career as well as the direction of the United States in the middle of the twentieth century. As president, Eisenhower told the 1958 graduating class at the United States Naval Academy, "Basic to our democratic civilization are the principles and convictions that have bound us together as a nation. Among these are personal liberty, human rights, and the dignity of man. All these have their roots in a deeply held religious faith—in a belief in God."

He believed in those values so much that he recommended to Congress and in 1954 signed the resulting bill to include the words "Under God" in the national Pledge of Allegiance.

Chapter Eight

Mistakes, Mishaps and Mischief

The American frontier was an unforgiving land. Life was tough, with daily challenges just to survive until the next day. Often times, play was equally as rough as children found release in activities that were sometimes as dangerous as their surrounding environment. Tools of everyday life—guns, hatchets, knives, conveyances, and horses—were so common that children went about their activities with little thought to the consequences of their use.

Parks and playgrounds remained rare in frontier communities, so children played where they could. Without modern precautions like fencing around construction sites, railroad yards, or businesses, youngsters could roam where their curiosity led them, sometimes with disastrous results. The natural inquisitiveness and immature foresight of pintsized pioneers often led them to dangerous predicaments that created opportunities for mistakes, mishaps, and mischief. Hazards occurred in everyday activities like playing baseball or football, pulling pranks, handling weapons, or going swimming.

"When fate consigns the small boy to a place where he can't go swimming, she robs him of half the joy of living," remembered John Taylor Waldorf years after his Virginia

City, Nevada, childhood. He and his friends swam in the "C&C pond," a gathering pool of water used in the mining process. The Consolidated Virginia and California Mining Companies, the latter of which produced forty-four million dollars in ore between 1876 and 1881, shared the pond. Another young male who used similar mining ponds for his aquatic recreation said the sediment-rich waters were "more like mud-crawling than swimming."

Just swimming in the C&C pond was mischief for Waldorf, whose parents prohibited it because "the impression prevailed in the family circle that I was born to be drowned," Waldorf recalled. Whenever he asked to go swimming, his father answered with a singing verse:

> "Oh, Mother, May I go out to swim?"
> "Oh, yes, my darling daughter;
> "You may hang your clothes on a hickory limb,
> "But don't go near the water."

Remembered Waldorf, "I wasn't a darling daughter, and Dad couldn't sing any better than I could, which meant something unique in the way of discord, but his meaning was plain." Young Waldorf went swimming anyway, and only hoped his hair dried before he returned home so as not to give away his disobedience. His parental precautions about frontier swimming were common because of the danger of water to young children. Youngsters drowned in rivers, lakes and even washtubs in the Old West.

A November 1894 headline in the *Capital Journal* of Salem, Oregon, summed up the danger: "Mill Creek Claims Another Victim from Among the Children." Three-year-old Clarence Casey was playing with the son of Salem Mayor Thomas Milton Gatch behind the Gatch house. The two boys slipped from the yard to the bank of the creek. There, the two little fellows tossed sticks into the stream for their dog to fetch. Investigators believed Clarence was holding a rope attached to the dog's neck and was yanked into the water, where he fell into a hole four feet deep and never came up. When the mayor's son returned home, he was asked where his companion was and innocently responded, "He is in the water, and he won't come out." Adults rushed to the spot, and Clarence's mother pulled her son from the creek, but she and physicians could not revive the poor boy.

Four-year-old F. McCarthy was playing with his siblings in the family corral behind their house outside of Fort Garland, Colorado, when he slipped away to play on Trinchera Creek. Somehow, the little one fell into the water unseen by his playmates. When he was deemed missing, his parents began a search and found his body a hundred and fifty yards downstream from the corral.

In Globe, Arizona, eleven-year-old George Barclay Pendleton was playing hide-and-seek with other boys near the train depot. As he approached a hand-dug railroad well, Barclay slipped and fell into fifteen feet of water. Railroad personnel heard the splash and within minutes extracted him with grappling hooks and revived his breathing, but not his consciousness. Barclay was taken to his parents' home, where he died during the night despite the efforts of two doctors.

Outside Laporte, Colorado, a worker named Tinley returned to the camp of his family near the banks of the Jackson irrigation canal and called for his children. All but his two-year-old responded. Alarmed that his offspring did not answer, the father raced to the irrigation ditch in a plaintive search for his son. The missing child was reported to the sheriff's office in Fort Collins. Law officers began a hunt. The next day they found the boy's body four miles from the family's camp.

Near Sutro, Nevada, eighteen-month-old Winfred Crowley was playing with some other children around her home when her mother stepped next door to check on a neighbor. When Margaret Crowley returned, she could not find the toddler with the others as her little one had wandered off. After a search, the horrified mom found her toddler head down in a partially filled washtub on the back porch. Evidently, the child had fallen partially into the tub and lacked the strength to push back out. Noted, the news account, "the parents are well-nigh crazy" over the loss.

Not all water incidents ended tragically. Outside Canon City, Colorado, little Ruth Hubbell fell into the icy snowmelt of a local stream. Hearing the commotion of women and children, Ed Fowler raced to the site, jumping two fences, then plunging into the frigid waters "without a second thought," reported the *Canon City Record*. He grabbed the girl, and "when he reached the bank with the child, her face was purple. Another minute in the water would probably have proved fatal."

In Albany, Oregon, several small boys were playing around a street bridge over the Santiam Canal, when one of them fell in. Seeing the accident, local resident Mrs. Dune Rankin rushed to the overpass, reached over, and snatched the boy by the arm as he floated by. She pulled him out so quickly that he never choked on the water. He was, though, thoroughly scared and raced home to his mother.

In Picacho, Arizona, the four-year-old son of Julian Para lost his balance and fell into the swift-running Colorado River. Fourteen-year-old Josefa Gonzales heard his cries, seized a long willow pole and raced to the rescue. She waded into the river until the water was up to her armpits, then extended the shaft, and pulled him to safety.

Fifteen-year-old Charley Knust rescued a four-year-old girl who was playing on a wharf and then fell into Lake Union near Seattle. While two men stood on the dock trying to fish her out with a pole, Charley raced from a block away, dived into the water fully clothed, grabbed the drowning child and hauled her to safety.

While several small boys were playing baseball near the town ditch in Phoenix, Arizona, one lost his balance attempting to catch a ball thrown his way and fell into the water-filled gulley. An unknown passerby arrived just in time to save him from a watery death.

Baseball and football, to a lesser extent, were played on the frontier, but not without hazards to players, spectators, and passersby. With many frontier communities lacking amenities like parks or playgrounds, boys started ballgames wherever they could find an open space, often in the street or on open and sometimes dangerous property. Such was the case in a pair of 1891 incidents in Montana mining country. In Helena, two teams were playing next to the Stevens mine with an unused, unfenced, and open shaft nearby. While the open shaft had once been covered with boards, the planks had been pilfered for firewood and never replaced. As sixteen-year-old Willie Corette was fielding a high fly, he forgot his proximity to the pit and fell fifty feet down the shaft, breaking his neck and his mother's heart. Similarly, in Butte during a Sunday afternoon baseball game, fifteen-year-old Willie Jones was likewise chasing a high fly ball and ran headlong into another open shaft, this one a hundred feet deep. Jones, too, died from the fall, one more casualty of baseball and shortsighted mine management.

As early as 1877, citizens of Golden, Colorado, were complaining about the practice of youngsters with bats and balls in the streets. Wrote the newspaper, "Golden objects to boys playing baseball in the business streets." By 1883, similar recreational activities drew the attention of authorities and the *Santa Fe New Mexican*, which noted, "The police have instructions to arrest all boys caught playing ball in the public streets." A decade later in Sioux Falls, South Dakota, the *Argus-Leader* reported, "Complaint comes to this office that boys playing football in the street are very careless about scaring [wagon] teams and are also reckless about running in front of the teams." The *Spectator* in Wetmore, Kansas, reported a farmer's complaint about boys playing ball on the streets. "He says his team always acts ugly when they see the boys playing ball. The boys should go off the main street to play ball."

The recreational practice was dangerous to life and property. In 1896 Lawrence, Kansas, Mrs. C.C. Irvin was out for a leisurely Friday evening carriage ride when she "met with a serious accident," according to the *Lawrence Weekly World*. As she drove past some boys playing in the street, a stray ball "hit the horse Mrs. Irvin was driving, causing it to run away." The matron flew from her carriage and sustained serious injuries "that may prove fatal." The paper editorialized, "This accident was caused by the small boys playing ball on the street, something the city cannot afford to tolerate. It is a wholly bad practice, and these boys ought to be arrested and other boys kept from endangering the lives of our citizens. While this is the first accident of the kind, there has been no end of complaints, and something ought to be done at once."

In a similar incident reported in the *Chickasaw Chieftain* in 1894, Oklahoma Territory, a Dr. and Mrs. Bell were driving through town in their buggy with their three-month-old infant in his mother's lap. They were compelled to go through a crowd of boys playing ball when one of the boys accidentally knocked a ball into the buggy, striking the baby in the head, nearly fracturing its skull. This case came very near being a fatal one and is a forerunner of what may be expected to follow if the great national game is allowed to be played upon public thoroughfares." The paper said, "It is now fully demonstrated beyond any doubt whatever that a stop should be put to the boys playing ball on any of the streets in the city."

The *Albuquerque Journal* agreed, writing in 1887, "The practice of ball-playing on the business streets is a very dangerous one, and parents should deter their children from indulging in it. Yesterday, while a number of boys were playing catch ball on Gold Avenue, the ball went crashing through a seventy-five dollar plate glass in A.M. Codington's furniture establishment. Two of the boys, named Concannon and Sanders, reported the accident to their parents, who assured Mr. Codington that they would see the damage liquidated."

By 1890, frontier communities began to take concerted action against the bad boys of baseball in Rapid City, South Dakota. Reported the *Black Hills Weekly Journal*, "Marshal McElroy yesterday rounded up a number of boys for playing ball upon the streets, and after giving them some good advice on the subject, and extracting a promise from them that in the future they would confine their ball-playing to the park or some other suitable place, let them go. The practice is a bad one and has been the cause of two or three runaways this season. Complaint having been made to the mayor a few days ago by a party whose horse had been frightened from this cause, he gave the marshal positive instructions to stop the practice, and should he have occasion to warn the parties a second time to do it after he had arrested them. So boys, look out, for should the marshal catch you playing ball in the streets, he will have you up before the city justice to be dealt with."

In Phoenix, the *Arizona Republic* agreed something needed to be done and looked to a community with a violent reputation for the solution. "Tombstone," wrote the paper, "has an ordinance requiring all boys under fifteen years of age to leave the streets after eight o'clock. As the town clock strikes the hour, boys playing on the streets can be seen hurrying home. It is a good ordinance and one that should be adopted in every town in the territory."

In a letter to the editor of the *Daily Oklahoman*, a citizen in 1894 wrote a facetious missive to the paper. "I would like to ask the officers of our city if wagons and buggies are to be banished from streets and business suspended during the balance of the season in favor of the ballplayers that infest our streets. You cannot drive a half dozen blocks without encountering a dozen groups of men or boys playing ball. A lady or child dare not attempt to drive down Main or Broadway in the evening for fear of the ballplayers. Is it not time for our city council or other authorities to recover the use of the streets and turn them over to their legitimate uses? There is room on the reservation for ball-playing, and it should be prohibited on our thoroughfares. Trusting that this will gain attention, I am A Horse Driver."

"A good deal of kicking is being done on the boys playing ball on the streets," reported the *Daily Traveler* in Arkansas City, Kansas, in 1895. "Delivery men and other persons who are compelled to drive a great deal say that half the streets in town are occupied by boys playing ball. The boys ought to vacate the streets and use the unoccupied lots for their games."

Not all the news of boys playing ball in the street was negative. In the case of an 1874 New Orleans report, it was downright amazing to see "a bevy of boys playing baseball with a dog in capacity of catcher." According to the local *Times*, "For half an hour during which we witnessed this novel game of baseball, the dog did not miss the ball a single time. And more than this, when, at our request, one of the boys threw the ball into the grass for a distance of about fifty feet, his canine catcher found it in an instant, and brought it back. The dog is evidently trained for the national game, and may yet make his mark as the champion catcher in this city."

Boys threw more than just baseballs in city streets. In Ogden, Utah, the local newspaper in 1874 reported, "Some boys were playing in the street, yesterday, and commenced throwing stones at a mule, when one of the stones struck a little boy named Stanford, knocking six of his teeth out and breaking the upper jaw." A similar complaint was raised by the *Deseret News* in Salt Lake City a year later. "Last Saturday evening the danger of throwing rocks, indulged in by many of our boys, was painfully illustrated. Some boys were playing near the residence of Mr. John Reeve, when a large stone was thrown in play, but it struck a son of Mr. Reeve, fourteen years of age, in the face, breaking his nose and inflicting a wound over the eye. The injured boy is in a fair way of speedy recovery, but the danger of this practice might have received a fatal illustration, and this should be a warning to the juveniles."

The *Daily Reporter* in Independence, Kansas, laid the blame on parents, writing, "A number of parents of this city seem careless of their children. There are a large number of them on the streets day and night, and it is a wonder that they are not injured more than they are. Take a drive over the city, and you will find children playing in the middle of the street who will never move when they see a horse coming, but will make a person drive around them. Then again there is another class of children, about nine-year-old boys—who are perambulating the streets at all times of the night. Parents keep your children at home. If you don't they will come to some bad end or be injured for life."

In Fort Worth, an 1893 *Daily Gazette* reporter posed the following questions in the headline: "Whose Streets? Do They Belong to the People of Fort Worth or to Special Occupants?" He complained about boys playing marbles in the street, speeding horses and buggies, unhitched horses, and other problems in violation of city ordinances. "Another dangerous feature of driving over the streets of Fort Worth is the number of little children playing in the streets, who have very narrow escapes from death under the hooves of the horses and wheels of the buggies. Then, these little children throw rocks at the buggies and, in some instances, inflict injuries upon the occupants. It takes a brave man or woman to drive over the streets of Fort Worth," concluded the reporter.

Frontier children played everywhere, not just in the streets. Without modern sensibilities and safeguards that today seem obvious and with parents preoccupied with survival, children often roamed wherever their curiosity took them. Further, with fencing expensive, many businesses and industrial sites did not install barriers to keep children and thieves out. Firms like lumberyards and construction companies had worksites where their inventories were open to anyone with a childhood curiosity or a felonious intent, both during and after business hours.

Little Joey Patterson was playing on the scaffolding of a new stone building under construction in St. Johns, Arizona, when he slipped and fell on a pile of building stones below. The accident left him unconscious for a while and sporting a three-inch gash on his head as well as badly bruised hands and some suspected internal injuries. He survived, however. Thirteen-year-old Tommy Boone fractured both arms at his wrists and badly scarred his face in a twenty-five-foot fall into a viaduct being built in Cheyenne, Wyoming. It seems the Boone lad and a friend used a plank to rig an impromptu seesaw atop a girder over the viaduct. In the process, Boone lost his balance and crashed back to earth.

Mills could be dangerous as well. In San Bernardino, California, the ten-year-old son of the Rincon flour mill manager was playing with friends among the whirling machinery when he got too near the cogwheels, which dragged him between the belting and the drum, crushing him and stopping all the machinery until he could be extricated. He lived but nine hours after the accident. In the Black Hills of South Dakota, six-year-old Georgie Andrews was playing around the Highland Mill when somehow the blocks securing a prone smokestack in place were dislodged. The smokestack rolled over the little fellow, who lived for five minutes after the accident. A passel of boys were romping around a pile of lumber outside a mill in the South Dakota mining town of Terraville, when they knocked over the pile. The plank avalanche broke seven-year-old Johnnie Adams's leg in two places and caused serious internal injuries. Boys playing on a stack of lumber in front of the Hotel Hamilton in Laredo, Texas, left the stack in such disarray that the *Laredo Times* noted the heavy pieces were "displaced and occupy a very dangerous position. This lumber should be straightened before it falls and perchance hurts some child."

The *Herald-Advance* of Milbank, South Dakota, reported on an 1893 lumberyard fatality in nearby Browns Valley. Young Herbert Felling, with his brother and several other boys were playing in the Dezotel and Smith lumberyard, when Herbert hid between two five-foot piles of drop-siding. When other boys climbed one of the stacks, they knocked over the siding, which crushed the boy.

Boys playing in lumberyards were common in the West, drawing the observations of the *Greenwood County Republican* in Eureka, Kansas, in 1890. Reported the paper, "Every Sunday the lumberyards are thronged with boys playing at hide-and-seek, thereby yelling and hollering, driving those in the neighborhood nearly distracted. They not only annoy the people, but they also smoke and might set fire to the lumber. Also in rainy weather, their muddy feet are tracked all over the boards, spoiling the sale, etc. We think the marshal might forbid such doings, as the Sabbath ought to be kept quiet even though the children do not attend Sunday school."

In an act of vandalism that became murder, a throng of boys in Portland knocked the supports out from under an unoccupied frame dwelling house. According to the *Oregonian*, the abandoned dwelling "came down with a crash, smashing into pieces, burying a number of the boys in the ruins." Fourteen-year-old Charles M. Beach died instantly, and eleven-year-old Martin Reddington was seriously injured, as was James Flanders. The three boys were using the empty dwelling as a clubhouse and were playing cards inside at the time of the accident, according to Portland's *Oregonian*.

Duty or curiosity could draw children to the rooftops of dwellings. A ball stuck on a roof drew a seven-year-old atop a house in Salt Lake City, but before he could retrieve the plaything, he slipped and fell sixteen feet to the ground. Though he badly bruised his face and head, he escaped with no broken bones. In another Salt Lake City incident, a twelve-year-old boy identified with the last name of Moore was playing atop a stable with other boys when he slipped and fell, garnering "a frightful gash" across his cheek.

Gravity was neither a child's rooftop nor riverbank friend. Two small children playing on a stream bank near Demersville, Montana, were caught in a landslide that carried them down the slope and almost buried them until their terrified cries brought rescuers who saved them. A similar accident occurred in Vernon, Texas, in 1890 with fatal results. Six small boys—three Baskerville brothers and three Wammock brothers—were playing in a sand bank when it caved in atop them. All six died.

Some hazards were not of the children's making. The *Tucson Citizen* in 1895 complained of all the abandoned wells and pits that lined the roadsides in southern Arizona. "Not only children playing in that direction but travelers at night accidentally straying from the road are liable to fall in, and unless it is some prominent party who is missed, the world is no wiser for their absence," noted the newspaper. The *Citizen* had previously reported on the menace of rotten telegraph and telephone poles around Tucson itself. "They have been in the ground for ten years and are rotted almost entirely off. A short time since one fell on Camp Street; another fell on Pennington and barely missed killing some children playing in the street."

Other fatal attractions for children young and old were trains, railroad tracks, and railroad yards. Rail property was full of things to climb or crawl under. Even turntables, which were used to change directions for locomotives, could serve as industrial merry-go-rounds if enough children had the strength to push them. Despite warnings from parents, teachers, rail employees, and local authorities, children still gravitated to the sound of the clickety-clack, often with dangerous outcomes.

In March 1874, the *Austin American-Statesman* described the problem succinctly: "Police!—Too many boys playing about the freight cars at the depot." The *Lawrence Daily Gazette* in 1890 Kansas elaborated more on what it called a "Dangerous Sport" as follows: "The practice of boys playing about moving trains in the railroad yards of Lawrence is a question that has agitated the minds of the agents for years, but there does not seem to be any decrease in the number who practice this dangerous sport. Engineer Moore, who pulls the Southern Kansas train between Ottawa and Lawrence, stated to a reporter this morning that every day when he enters and leaves the Lawrence yards, a crowd of boys plays on the track from the depot to the Carbondale track. He says that they get in front of the engine and remain there until the engine almost strikes them. 'Someday' said Mr. Moore, 'they will get in each other's way and the engine will strike and kill one and perhaps two or three of them. We use every precaution the railroad provides to prevent accidents, but I am afraid every time I pass through the Lawrence yards that I will kill some of those boys'."

Both boys and girls wound up injured or worse during playtime near railroads. A Wabash work train at Camden, Missouri, ran over six-year-old Ora West and the ten- and eight-year-old Van Horn brothers, who were playing on the track. "They were mangled beyond recognition," reported the *Kingfisher Times* in Oklahoma Territory. At a station in Bunceton, Missouri, a crowd of boys was playing on a sidetrack when a freight car rolled over fifteen-year-old Albert Dixon, cutting him in half. Nine-year-old Benigno Baca was hit by a freight train in Wagon Mound, New Mexico, and sustained fatal injuries. News accounts said, "Nothing could be done for him further than to relieve pain with opiates." He died within two hours of the accident. Such fatalities were numerous and recorded throughout the American West.

Many railroad injuries resulted as well, including three-year-old Bessie Chipman of American Fork, Utah. She and two little female companions were playing on the Union Pacific track. The engineer mistook the children for a calf lying between the rails and blew his whistle to scare the supposed animal away. When he saw two girls scamper away, he thought they had left an item of clothing behind. It was Bessie. She tried to scamper away, but her foot got stuck. It was severed in the accident, but Bessie survived.

In Flagstaff, Arizona, Manuel Madero "had a miraculous escape from a horrible death," according to a local newspaper. He was playing on the tracks before he realized a train was bearing down on him. The cowcatcher on the front of the locomotive pushed him off the track, but one hand fell on a rail, and little Manuel lost three fingers. Fifteen-year-old Norman Evans was playing on a railcar in Emporia, Kansas, when a switch engine bumped it down the track, throwing him on the rails and stunning him. His pal Harry Logston saw what happened and grabbed Evans, jerking him from the tracks but not in time to prevent the engine from hitting him, breaking both of his legs and an arm.

In Salt Lake City, several small boys were placing nails on the track to let passing railcars and locomotives flatten them. When a switch engine passed, the boys raced to get their "scissors," as they called the flattened nails, not noticing a boxcar rolling behind. One of the unidentified youth was struck in the head, cutting a long gash and fracturing his skull. The boy survived. The *Richfield Advocate* in Utah in 1896 identified the town's "first railroad casualty" as twelve-year-old Andrew Lawson, who was playing with one of the smaller railroad construction carts, pushing it up and down the track. Young Lawson tripped, and one of the small wheels rolled over his foot, dislocating his ankle. In Salt Lake City, five-year-old Constance Nielson was playing under some rail cars when the train started to move. In trying to get from under the train, she rolled over a rail, but her left foot was frightfully crushed and required amputation.

The difficulty of determining responsibility for the accidents was illustrated by an 1897 inquest into the death of Andrew Maffei, approximately ten years old, in Meaderville, Montana. Andrew and his younger brother Angelo were playing on a coal car when it started to roll down an incline. As the car picked up speed, Andrew yelled, "Mama, Mama," then fell onto the tracks and was crushed. The question before the inquest was whether faulty brakes were at fault, or whether Angelo had released them. After a day and a half of witnesses, the inquest decided Angelo had used a tack hammer to loosen the brakes so the car would roll. Left unanswered was the question of whether Angelo had released the brakes accidentally or intentionally to give his brother a thrill.

On occasion, train passengers were injured by children. Near the depot at Oneida, Kansas, boys playing with a slingshot sent a rock through the window of an eastbound Santa Fe train, striking Mrs. Will Mayo in the eye, blinding her in that eye.

Though many tragedies were reported about pintsized pioneers and trains in the newspapers, occasionally a funny story appeared in the papers, like the two little boys playing in a Southern Pacific train yard near San Francisco. Realizing they were thirsty, they decided to get a drink from the water tank used to fill the steam locomotives. As the San Francisco paper reported, one "boy got directly under the nozzle, threw his head back, and opened his mouth like a young robin" while his pal yanked the rope. Continued the news account, "Swash! A small boy lay on the ground gasping for breath. A stream of water a foot in diameter was fast hammering him out of sight into the ground, when some yard hands went to his rescue."

In addition to manmade perils, Mother Nature threw hazards at playing youngsters, lightning strikes being the most deadly and unpredictable. In Cedar Valley, Utah, little Lee Cook and Howard Rodeback were playing in the loft of the Cook barn when lighting struck, "the thunderbolt suddenly came like an explosion, demolishing one corner of the barn, just a few feet from where the boys were standing," according to newspaper reports. The shock knocked both boys to the floor, but what made the strike unusual was that it came with the sun shining brightly and only a few clouds in the sky.

In Waco, Texas, during a spring thunderstorm, lightning struck a dwelling, coming down the stovepipe and passing across the floor like a ball of fire, and severely shocking the children playing in the room. Another bolt struck close to several youngsters running around the public school yard that day, stunning a boy named Frank Tennant so severely that he was carried home unconscious, but recovered later in the day.

During a thunderstorm near Plattsburg, Missouri, lightning struck the home of Mrs. John McClelland and killed her while she was working at her sewing machine. Her three little children, playing in the same room at the time, escaped unscathed. In Las Vegas, New Mexico Territory, during a summer day, four boys were romping in an arroyo when a sudden storm came up and loosed a bolt of lightning, killing one and stunning his playmates. Six children playing on the veranda at their home were knocked out by a July lightning bolt. One later died, and two others remained in critical condition in Lovelady, Texas.

Near Hubbard Chapel, Texas, one August afternoon, several men and boys were playing a game of baseball when a sudden shower came up. The throng gathered under a tree for protection from the rain when a lightning bolt struck their wooden shelter and knocked down seventeen men and youths. Of that number, seven died, four were seriously injured, and the others received severe shocks. The dead included one father of four. The rest of the fatalities were youths or boys.

Another natural hazard to children and animals was hail, best exemplified by an 1878 storm that did more than ten thousand dollars in damage in and around Cheyenne, Wyoming. Reported the town's *Democrat Leader*, "The first warning the people had of the coming storm was a loud roaring in the north, followed by a strong wind, and then came the storm of hail." Four little boys playing near the Union Pacific tracks were caught outside in the storm. Eugene Callahan was struck on the head by a huge hailstone, cutting a gash two inches long into the skull. Another boy by the name of Ryder was "wounded about the head and body in a fearful manner." Joe Perry sustained several injuries, one hailstone striking him on the arm, nearly breaking it. "Returning home after the storm had abated, they presented to their anxious parents a gory spectacle," reported the newspaper, which noted, "The size of the hailstones that fell were astonishingly large, some of them measuring nine inches and a half in circumference, and weighing several ounces." That circumference translates to a hailstone three inches in diameter.

As if the weather was not enough, horses presented a constant danger. Equines were so ever-present that children and adults took them for granted. Two little girls were playing in a Guthrie, Oklahoma Territory, buggy when the horse broke away, tossing the girls free and damaging the rig before the horse was stopped. In Salem, Oregon, young Paul Bower and several friends were having a good time in a vacant lot with a horse, which ended the frivolity by "lifting both hind heels and sending them out with terrific force," reported the local newspaper. "One of them landed on the bridge of Paul's nose, breaking it down, making a deep cut above one eye, and fracturing the cheekbone." Doctors remained uncertain whether they could save the imperiled eye. In nearby Albany, Oregon, a horse kicked a little girl with the last name of Montague while she played with the rope tethering him. According to the *Albany Weekly Herald*, "The little girl was knocked about twenty feet distant. One hoof struck her on the mouth and the other on her leg, but strange to say, beyond a few bruises the child was not much hurt."

In South Dakota near Alkali, brothers George McPherson, age fifteen, and Glen McPherson, age twelve, were herding cattle and playing with each other, trying to toss lariats attached to their saddle pommels over one another. According to newspaper accounts, "Glen succeeded in getting the rope on his brother, Eugene, when the pony took fright and started off on a mad run. For two miles, the unfortunate boy was dragged over rocks, hills, and gullies until death came to his relief. When found, the body was a sad sight to look upon."

While a youth in Fillmore City, Utah, was recklessly racing his horse down a main street in town, he burst through a bunch of playing boys, running over eight-year-old Thomas Wade, who died the next day from the injuries. In Basin, Idaho, a nine-year-old boy with the last name of Fairchild was playing with some friends around a haystack with a horse tied to a wagon nearby. When young Fairchild attempted to pass between the haystack and the wagon, the horse kicked him near the top of the forehead over the left eye, making an ugly wound and fracturing his skull. Reported the newspaper, "The little fellow now lies in a critical condition. Hopes are entertained for his recovery, but the prospect is not at all favorable."

In Rowena, Oregon, four-year-old Ruth Webber was playing about the street when a farmer's frightened team knocked her down and dragged the loaded wagon over her, breaking five ribs and leaving the little girl spitting blood. In Grand Forks, North Dakota, a four-year-old child, one of several romping in the streets, was crushed by a heavy wagon pulled by a runaway team. The little one died half an hour later.

Six-year-old Carlos Kumpe was riding on the tongue of a freight wagon in Diamond City, Montana, when he fell off. Two wheels of the wagon loaded with thirty-five hundred pounds of freight rumbled over his thighs. "Strange to say, however, no bones were broken; the flesh was somewhat bruised, but the injuries are slight in comparison to what might have been expected," reported the *Rocky Mountain Husbandman*. "The escape was fortunate, but the circumstance should be a warning to children playing on the streets not to play about teams."

Beyond the injuries and fatalities, runaways caused many narrow escapes. In Pittsburg, Kansas, a runaway horse and buggy charged down a local road where "a number of children playing in the road barely escaped being run over," according to the *Daily Headlight*. One Monday evening in Brenham, Texas, a dozen loose horses charged down Main Street past the northwest corner of the courthouse square and a throng of boys playing in the street. "A fatal accident seemed imminent," reported the *Weekly Banner*, "but fortunately they escaped, though the horses had to jump almost directly over one of them."

While nature and horses could be threats, some children brought problems on themselves with their pranks. Halloween became a common occasion for mischief. During one such occasion in Salt Lake City, a crowd of venturesome young males thought they would steal a table from the front of merchant C.E. Fisher's store. "The proprietor promptly fired two shots in their direction," chronicled the *Salt Lake Herald*. "The boys scattered." In Lead, South Dakota, one Halloween night, boys "marked up a great number of show windows" in the local stores. The *Daily Call* noted, "The merchants were busy this morning cleaning the same. There is no loss without some gain as all the windows along Main Street present a brand new appearance this afternoon."

Some pranks were pure meanness and vandalism, such as in 1898 Prescott, Arizona, when pranksters overturned a windmill, causing fifty dollars in damage, and shot a horse on Halloween. In Hillsboro, New Mexico Territory, three boys from prominent families were spotted killing a goat belonging to a ranchman. "Warrants for the arrest of the amateur butchers were sworn out," reported the *Santa Fe New Mexican*, "and now the boys are playing hide-and-seek with the officers."

While many accidental fires were caused by children playing with matches, other instances saw blazes started as pranks. In Salt Lake City, some male vandals set fire to an outhouse, doing twenty dollars in damage. Two small boys desiring to see firemen put out a fire, lit a four-acre pasture of grassland inside the Portland city limits. Neighbors poured out of nearby homes and fought the blaze with old sacks, brooms, and pieces of brush until the fire wagon arrived and connected hoses to a nearby hydrant. The fire burned an acre and a half of the tract before it "yielded to its watery foe. It gave that neighborhood a sound fright, and it is to be hoped taught the young scamps a salutary lesson," observed the *Oregonian*.

Some pranks were criminal, like the case of Vernal, Utah, postmaster and storekeeper Louis Allen, who kept losing change from his register when he went to his home nearby for lunch. Though he did not lock his front door, he attached a line from the entrance to his home so that a bell would ring when the door was opened. One day, he marked some coins and went to lunch, but returned quicker than usual. He discovered the money missing, but saw two boys playing in the street. When he accused them of the thefts, "which they stoutly denied at first but finally breaking down, they confessed their guilt," reported the *Salt Lake Herald*. Knowing the door was linked to a bell at Allen's home, the twelve- and thirteen-year-old boys had crawled in through the window to steal the change. "An effort will be made to have them sentenced to the reform school," the paper reported.

Sometimes, though, the prankster's conscience weighed on the perpetrator, which was the only explanation Portland, Oregon, storeowner C.E. Kelley could come up with when a display window was smashed and then a door window broken so a burglar could enter. The perplexing thing about the 1895 break-in was that nothing was taken. In thinking through the odd situation, Kelley remembered a pack of boys rolling and throwing stones outside his store the evening of the illicit entry. Kelley concluded the boys had accidentally thrown a rock through his window and realized they could get in trouble for the breakage. Therefore, they broke the door window so they could unlock the entry, slip inside, retrieve the rock, and remove any evidence they had broken the glass.

On other occasions, the pranksters had to be shamed into correcting the wrong, as in the case of an incident reported in the 1887 *Kimball Enterprise* of South Dakota. A trio of schoolboys was awaiting the start of morning classes when they saw an old man pass by with a load of potatoes in the back of his wagon as he approached a hill. One of them suggested it would be fun to release the wagon's tailgate so the tubers would slide out on the road.

The trio succeeded in their mischievous mission without the old man discovering their prank. Not so their teacher, who watched the whole incident just as the school bell rang. As the students sat down, and before she called roll, the teacher said, "As I came into the schoolhouse, I saw an old man picking up potatoes from the dusty road, and I want to tell you something about him. At the beginning of the Civil War, he and his only son, a young man of twenty-three, enlisted in the army and fought in many battles, until at Gettysburg he was dangerously wounded and his son killed.

"It was six months before he could leave the hospital to come home, and what he suffered in trying to live and get well cannot be told. Since that time, he has had many aches and pains, and it has been very hard for him to earn enough to support his wife and himself. He is very lame and has to move slowly. It will take him a long time to pick up his potatoes. People say that he never did a mean thing in his life, and he is the kindest man I know."

At that point, one miscreant raised his hand, and volunteered to go pick up the potatoes if he could be dismissed from class for the task. Before the teacher answered, his two accomplices agreed they would like to help as well. When the boys reached the old man, he was resting by the wagon from the tedious chore. They admitted they had caused the problem. "Now, if you will sit down in the shade of that tree," the repenting leader announced, "We will pick up all your potatoes for you."

The elderly veteran placed his trembling hand upon the head of the boy and looked from him to the other two. "My dear boys, you have done a brave thing. Never be ashamed to tell the truth or confess a fault."

With that, the man sat down and watched the three boys right their mischief. After completing the task, the boys returned to their classroom. Saying nothing, the teacher merely smiled, knowing the boys had learned a lesson more important than anything else on the curriculum that day.

Chapter Nine

Toys and Dolls

From the beginning of time, boys and girls have played with dolls and toys, even if they had to make them or find everyday substitutes that served the purpose in their imaginations. It was no different on the early American frontier, where toys and dolls were often primitive, but nonetheless fulfilled the playtime needs of children and their fantasies. The availability of toys during the first half of the frontier era between 1840 and 1870 was much more limited in the West than during the second half from 1871 to 1900. Thanks both to the nation's expanding web of western railroads and to the lower prices of mass-produced consumer goods, toys became more economical and more readily available everywhere.

According to federal census records, forty-seven American toy manufacturers operated in the nation in 1850. Three decades later, the number of U.S. toy producers had more than tripled, totaling one hundred and seventy-three. Technological improvements made sheet-metal stamping feasible for producing economical tin toys and soldiers in mass quantities for pintsized boys. New molding machines and techniques resulted in more lifelike dolls for little girls. Enhanced printing procedures provided more colorful packaging options to appeal to both children and parents.

The rise of Chicago mail-order catalog companies, starting with Montgomery Ward and Company in 1872 and Sears, Roebuck, and Company in 1892 made mass-produced toys affordable and accessible in all but the most remote parts of the country. Until the implementation of Rural Free Delivery in 1896, countryside residents had to pick up their catalogs in their community post offices. After the U.S. Post Office started RFD, the catalogs were delivered directly to rural mailboxes along with the other mail.

Montgomery Ward issued its first "catalog" in 1872, a single-page that listed one hundred and sixty-three items for sale. A quarter of a century later, the Montgomery Ward catalog had expanded to over six hundred pages and more than twenty-five thousand items for sale, everything from toys to tools, from furniture to farm machinery, and from dolls to diamonds. The catalogs were dream books not only for children but also for their parents, who could aspire to purchase more of the merchandise the more they prospered. Once a new edition arrived, little girls could use the previous one to cut out the paper figurines and other toy items. The outdated catalogs also had a more practical use as well. In many rural homes, pages from the catalog were used as toilet paper in outdoor privies, a practice that continued in rural regions well into the twentieth century and the Great Depression.

Before the spread of the railroads and the rise of the mail-order catalogs, children were left to their own devices for playthings. Youthful imaginations reigned. In west Texas, one little girl furnished her makeshift dollhouse with pottery shards for furniture and a cow patty for an imaginary piano. In the Flint Hills of Kansas, young girls constructed make-believe dollhouses out of bleached bones remaining from the slaughter of buffalo herds in the region. Some girls in especially poor families used crook-necked squash for dolls. For doll clothes, little lasses like Allie Wallace in Oklahoma Territory used cottonwood leaves to "sew" doll clothing and hats.

Many a frontier boy built miniature wagons from empty pill or cartridge boxes, spools, buttons, and twine, imitating their parents' farm vehicles or those of the ever-present freighters who delivered goods before the railroad arrived. In Kansas, a brother and sister made several such tiny wagons and harnessed large locusts to the rigs to make a freight caravan. Just north in Nebraska, two sisters created two families of corncob dolls whose imaginary lives paralleled their own, living in dugouts and working in the fields. Likewise, in Texas, a young boy created his own diminutive ranching empire with a flock of popcorn for his sheep and a herd of pecans for his cattle. Sioux City, Iowa, playmates Willie Durgan and Albert Saxby spent hours playing along the bank of the Missouri River, making playhouses out of driftwood. Scraps of lumber were used as building blocks or whatever else little minds could imagine throughout the West.

Born in 1896 Kansas, young William Allen White made many of his toys, some as simple as whistles, stick horses, and bows and arrows. Other of White's homemade playthings were more complicated, like a sled, a wagon, and a little railroad "with whittled ties." An 1866 San Francisco native who grew up in Sacramento, California, with his well-to-do parents, Lincoln Steffens dreamed of being a teamster, a gunfighter, a bronc buster, and a steamboat man. In his riverboat imitations, Steffens removed a leaf from the family dining table, placed it on the floor, kneeled on it, and rocked it back and forth across the carpet to traverse the room, all the while tooting like a steamboat whistle. As an imaginary freighter, he lined up small chairs—his team of horses—in front of three or four bigger chairs—his freight wagons. Steffens next tied a cord to his first chair or horse and ran it through the backs of the other chairs as "a rein which I could jerk as the black-bearded teamsters did."

Eight-year-old David Siceloff in Oklahoma's Cherokee Strip decided he needed "a little wagon to play with," so he and a friend scrounged the materials for the project. "We hunted up nails, pieces of board, lath, and anything we could get hold of that we might use," he recalled. "Shop was set up in the barn, and we worked like beavers." They assembled front and rear axles, wagon box, tongue, bows, wagon sheet, and makeshift wheels. When completed, he and his pal considered it "the finest covered wagon to be found in all the Strip." However, once it was completed, the two boys had little time to play with it because of their chores. Concluded Siceloff, "It was more fun making it than playing with it."

Young girls also relished making their own toys. On the Kansas prairie, Hannah Darrah recalled, "We children enjoyed playing in the clay of the river bank. We became quite expert in fashioning dishes, dolls, and whole herds of animals out of this clay, which we enjoyed quite as much as the children of today their squawking mama dolls."

Even something as simple as a ball was often made by hand, sometimes by siblings for gifts. On the Great Plains, young George Thompson remembered a baseball his older sister made for him by unraveling some worn woolen socks, then wrapping the strands around a wood fragment and covering it with a piece of leather. His sibling gave the homemade ball to him the Christmas after a plague of locusts had devastated the family farm. "No Christmas since," he later wrote, "with all its variety of presents no matter how valuable, has ever given me the joy and happiness of that little ball." Even simple toys and gestures left lasting memories out West.

In 1890s Creede, Colorado, young Edwin Lewis Bennett and his pal Harry enjoyed playing "Greeks and Trojans" rather than cowboys and Indians. To recreate the Trojan War from Greek mythology, the boys used curtain rods for spears and rigged a pair of discarded boiler lids with arm loops and handgrips for shields. Then they would stand outside and chunk their "spears" at each other as they re-fought the Trojan War in Colorado mining country. "Naturally, our accuracy improved with practice, and that was our downfall," Bennett remembered. "On an afternoon when both our mothers had to patch up some head wounds and contusions, we ceased to be Achilles and Menelaus and Paris and those other interesting citizens of Greece and Troy we had been imitating."

In Kansas, Charles Driscoll and his brothers played judge and jury one day, distraught that the county sheriff had not arrested and punished a local lawbreaker. The boys set up a miniature courtroom and conducted a trial for the misdemeanor defendant, in this case a baking powder can. After hearing the evidence, the jury returned a guilty verdict, and the accused was hanged. In Charles's recollection, the criminal "dangled in midair, at the end of a length of binder twine, a lesson in public morals for all the world to see." Juvenile justice could be hard on Old West miscreants, even those tin cans convicted of misdemeanors.

As most rural homes also had a barn to shelter livestock, tools, and farm equipment, the outbuilding became a favorite playing spot for children, a place where they could often escape their parents' supervision. In the imagination of youngsters, the barn could become a fort or a castle or even a schoolhouse. In Oklahoma Territory, young David Siceloff remembered, "When the barn was finished, the carpenters were paid off. A passing wagon took them and their tool chests and bedrolls to Pond Creek. I missed the sawing and hammering. The new barn became my favorite place to play. It was the only shady spot where one could run about, make covered wagons, skin animals, and escape from the weather. Behind the hay we could hide and watch for Indians—there were none— and horse thieves that we did not recognize when we saw them."

In Nebraska, young George MacGinitie played with homemade toys, often made or imagined by him. As store-bought toys were a luxury, little George treasured a clear glass marble with a silver rooster frozen in its center. "I carried this marble around by the hour," he recalled, "marveling at its structure and thrilled by its beauty." By the 1880s, with the railroad reaching more communities in the West, local stores featured more toys and trinkets. Further, once the Montgomery Ward catalog became more accessible throughout rural America, the choices for playthings among frontier children greatly expanded.

As an example, a November 1881 *Nevada State Journal* ad for Nasby's Bazaar in Reno, Nevada, stated, "Nasby has an endless variety of toys of every description. His goods were all purchased in the eastern market. His store is well-arranged for the coming holidays. At the Bazaar may be found dolls dressed, undressed, boy dolls, girl dolls, colored dolls, bisque dolls, indestructible dolls, and wax dolls; tin toys of every shape; A-B-C and building blocks made of walnut; ten pins, [piggy] banks, chimes, trumpets, writing desks, albums, and fine papeteries, etc."

With mass production, playthings became more sophisticated. Wooden building blocks, for instance, were no longer just plain wooden cubes. Now they were embossed with letters and numbers and painted in various colors. These refinements provided additional learning opportunities where little ones could study the alphabet, colors, and numbers while they stacked the pieces.

Mechanical piggy banks were popular—among parents for sure—because they taught youngsters the benefit of saving money, even if just a penny at a time. The kids loved them because the coins were thrown into the slot in various ways. For instance, the 1894-95 Montgomery Ward catalog offered an "Artillery Bank" where a penny was placed in a wide-mouth cannon, which was cocked and fired, sending the coin into an opening in a fort. In the "Baseball Bank," a coin was secured in the pitcher's hand and tossed at the push of a lever toward a batter who swings and misses as the money piece flies into the catcher's mitt, which is the opening of the bank. An "Eagle Bank" required children to put a coin in a mother eagle's beak. As the lever was pulled, the maternal bird leaned over and dropped the metal piece in the nest where two hungry eaglets awaited. A "Kicking Mule Bank" featured a rider who held the penny in his mouth until the switch was moved and the mule kicked its hind legs, tipping the rider forward to drop the penny in a receptacle. The mechanical banks provided an entertaining way for children to save money.

By the time of the 1894-95 Montgomery Ward catalog, the fifty-sixth since the mail-order firm began distributing the wish books, fifteen pages displayed toys, not including those advertising bicycles and sleds. Selections included various toy musical instruments such as harps for a dollar fifty, violins and bows for a quarter, little pianos from ninety cents to five dollars and toy drums—every parent's musical nightmare—for seventy-five cents to two dollars.

Reflecting the products of the Industrial Revolution, little boys could purchase iron and tin train sets, replicas of vertical and horizontal steam engines with prices starting at a quarter and going up to four-and-a-half dollars for a beam-and-mill engine. A selection of "indestructible malleable iron toys" included various carts, wagons, fire engines, hose-and-ladder carts, carriages, and freight wagons, some with a team and some without, for prices between forty cents and four dollars. Little boys could also choose from sets of tin and wooden soldiers from forty to ninety cents, toy army rifles with bayonets for a dollar, and pistols that shot darts with suction cups on the end for fifty cents.

By December 1897, even in the remote mining town of Bozeman, Montana, local youth had a wide selection of mass-produced toys. The Willson Company advertised "A World of Things for the Children. Hundreds of nice playthings that please the little ones, and cost but a song." A dime would buy a large box of blocks, a play watch with a chain or a large kaleidoscope. For a quarter, boys could acquire a twenty-inch-long tin monitor gunboat, a nickel-plated trumpet, a wooden or tin train of cars, a surprise box, various musical toys as well as fire engines or hook-and-ladder trucks, mechanical cats, monkeys, and a windup tin rowboat. Willson customers could buy a twenty-six-inch tin steamship, a train of cars with patent wheels, windup bicycles with "real rubber tires," tin trotting horses and sulkies, a two-horse grocery cart and road wagons for fifty to seventy cents. For a dollar or more, boys could secure a thirty-four-inch gunboat, a train with engine and six coaches, and a "fine train with multiple cars and complete tracks."

Some catalog offerings appealed to both boys and girls, such as a variety of gray or white rubber animal toys, ranging from a gray mouse at eighteen cents to a white cat with a whistle for fifty cents. Mass production also broadened the variety and types of games available, including the board variety. For eighty-five cents, lads could buy "The Yale-Harvard Game," a board game that simulated the emerging sport of college football. Then there was a similarly priced "The Limited Mail and Express Game," promoted as "the new, popular board game, elegantly produced and played upon a map of the United States with Miniature Railroad Trains, etc. The trains carry cotton from the South, tobacco from Virginia, corn from Iowa, livestock from Texas, etc., as well as mail matter from all parts of the country. It is extremely amusing."

"The Soldier Boy Game" was played on an almost two-feet-square folding board. It was described as "especially captivating for boys. With the game comes four metal soldiers and spinning indicator for playing. The game relates the stirring story of the battlefield and illustrates the promotion gained by ability, bravery, and ambition. The winner of the game is the player who first attains the position of Commander-in-Chief."

Most expensive of all the games listed in the 1894-95 catalog was "Across the Continent," described as "the most elaborate board game ever issued" with a playing surface twenty-one by forty-two inches and offering a "bird's-eye view" of the United States with the principal cities and railroad lines. According to the catalog description, "In the course of the game, players make a trip across the Continent and back, follow the routes stated on their tickets, and pay traveling expenses. Railway tickets, toy money, fine celluloid pieces, enameled cups, and full directions with each game. It has utensils for six players, but any number can play. It is an exciting and educational amusement."

Another educational amusement was the magic lantern, a forerunner of the early slide projectors and later silent movies. The lantern consisted of an illumination source in an enclosure with a sliding frame between the light and a lens, which projected images on the wall. Glass slides with illustrations and photographic images would be inserted in the frame, which was pulled through the box for viewing. Slides could be purchased with images of nursery tales, Mother Goose fables, landscapes, and cities from various countries. The upper-end lanterns themselves sold for from five to eight dollars in the Montgomery Ward catalog, while sets of slides went from thirty-five cents to a dollar-seventy-five for a dozen images. At the Willson Company in Bozeman, toy magic lanterns sold for seventy-five cents with six slides or a dollar-thirty-five for twelve slides.

While magic lanterns and various games appealed to both boys and girls, the young ladies migrated to more maternal and domestic toys. Girls could choose a variety of dishes and tea sets with Montgomery Ward catalog prices starting at twenty cents. Doll furniture was popular as well with everything from doll beds to doll swings to doll hammocks to doll high chairs, all for a dollar or less, depending upon the size. Other furniture items included bedroom sets, sewing machines, rocking chairs, and miniature blackboard stands, again most for a dollar or less. Two full pages of dolls were available for purchase with prices varying from forty cents for a thirteen-inch doll to three-and-a-quarter dollars for a twenty-one-inch figurine. Some dolls closed their eyes; others clapped. Others were dressed in the latest Victorian fashion of the era, while some came without clothes, which could be purchased separately. Those fashion accessories offered shoes, booties, stockings, corsets, hats, caps, dresses, cloaks, capes and more, with costs ranging from a dime to seventy-five cents.

More economical paper dolls could be acquired for twenty cents plus four cents postage. The lithographed dolls on heavy cardboard with an easel back came with "three dresses of different colors and styles with hats to match, packed in [a] neat box." For little girls who could not afford those paper dolls, they could cut out the figurine images in outdated catalogs.

Dolls were the most common and enduring of the manufactured toys. Before the fancy, mass-produced catalog dolls, pintsized lasses played with dolls made of cornhusks or corncobs, whittled out of wood, cut out of cloth and stuffed with sawdust, fashioned out of rags, and created in other ways limited only by a child's imagination. While dolls remained the domain of girls, many boys played with dolls until they neared adolescence. Nebraskan George MacGinitie had a younger brother who had several pet toads he treated as dolls, even fashioning doll clothes for them and calling them "doll toads."

By 1887, those old-style, homemade dolls were being replaced by the manufactured variety, so much so that the authors of *The American Girls Handy Book* suggested a nostalgic trip down dolly lane for their young readers with instructions for making cornhusk and flower dolls. Wrote the authors, "No such beautiful dolls as delight the hearts of the children of today ever peeped forth from the Christmas stockings of our grandmothers or great-grandmothers when they were little girls. In those times there were not, as there are now, thousands of people doing nothing but making toys for the entertainment and pleasure of the little ones, and the motherly little hearts were fain to content themselves with lavishing unlimited affection and care upon a rag, wooden, or cornhusk baby, made and dressed at home. Since then almost every child tired of, and surfeited with handsome and expensive toys, has been glad at times to get grandma to make for her a real old-fashioned dolly, which might be hugged in rapturous moments of affection without fear of dislocating some of its numerous joints, or putting out of order its speaking or crying apparatus; and might in times of forgetfulness be dropped on the floor and suffer no injury thereby." The authors suggested their grandmother's dolls were "just the kind to adopt for the summer" and to note that "the fine French doll with its delicate wax or china face, silky hair, and dainty toilets, is more suited to the elegances of the parlor than to the wear and tear of outdoor life" in the summer. The authors then provided little girls precise instructions on how to construct cornhusk dolls just like their grandmothers did.

Whether handmade or manufactured, dolls were ubiquitous on the frontier, likely the most popular toy not only in the West but also in the history of the world. An 1888 *Gazette* journalist in Rush Center, Kansas, described it this way: "So far as I have been able to discover, there's not a girl, from the huts of the north pole to the leaf tents of the equator—north, south, east, or west, who has not some sort of a doll. I doubt if there ever lived a girl in that desolate condition, for a bit of rolled-up rag, or a corncob, a long-necked squash or a stick of wood, is easily imagined to be all that the little owner desires, and is often far more tenderly loved and cherished than the finest French wax doll in the world. A poppy blossom or a hollyhock makes a charming doll; and I have seen a lovely one made and dressed from the tender inside husks of green corn."

By the late 1890s in Bozeman, the Willson Company advertised, "Dolls at wholesale prices. We buy Dolls as low as the largest in the country, and sell them to you as cheaply as other dealers pay for them." The store offered kid body dolls, "All with closing eyes, shoes and stockings and stout bodies," priced from a quarter for the thirteen-inch doll to a dollar fifty for the twenty-four-inch variety. They also advertised unbreakable dolls, felt body dolls, patent dolls with hair and glass eyes, and dressed dolls representing boys and girls, Indian maidens, Highland lassies, brides, blacks, Gypsies, Eskimos, and "swell young lady dolls, stunningly dressed in silks," priced from a nickel to two dollars and seventy-five cents.

Sanger Brothers' Store in 1898 Waco, Texas, advertised "DOLLS! DOLLS! What can you find to please the children with better than with dolls? Even in the wilds of Africa, you will find dolls of some description for the children to play with. Some are hideous and repulsive to our more refined and educated tastes, but they serve their purpose to amuse the children. In our Doll Department, you will find nothing repulsive, but a vast collection of attractively beautiful dolls—dolls that, when they become the possessors of them, will make your children proud as kings. Big Dolls, Little Dolls, Boy Dolls, Girl Dolls, Sailor Dolls, and Soldier Dolls—All dressed in the height of fashion, and in suitable combinations of colors. Large Jointed Dolls with bisque heads—large as baby herself. Any of them will delight a child as nothing else will."

With dolls a mainstay in the play of frontier youngsters, they helped children develop a protective empathy for the smaller and more helpless little ones among them. Dolls also provided a coping mechanism for youngsters to deal with the tragic realities of injury and death in frontier life. Sometimes dolls broken or damaged—accidentally or even intentionally—received their own funerals. Remembered one girl, "Doll broken, funeral just for fun." Another young girl recalled later in life playing with her doll Becky. "Funerals were especially popular, with Becky ever the willing victim." Such doll play helped youngsters to work through the all too common grief and tragedies of frontier life.

An Old West existence remained tough not only on children but also on their dolls, as reflected in 1889 by a *San Francisco Chronicle* reporter's visit to a doll repair shop. The writer published the tongue-in-cheek story as if he were taking a battered doll to a "doll hospital," where a German "surgeon-in-chief and two female assistants or nurses" attended the "patients."

"The hospital is a successful and well-patronized establishment," reported the visitor, "and the number of cases that have been conducted to a safe and happy conclusion is quite as large as can be shown by any other similar establishment. Indeed, the percentage of cures is a larger one than many hospitals of a much more extended reputation can boast of, and the patient who is given up as 'hopeless' must be in a very bad way indeed."

Inquiring about the most common maladies faced by dolls, the reporter learned from the doll doctor, "Dislocation, decapitation, depilation, denudation, degeneration, and general disorganization are about the most common diseases." In terms of accidents, the surgeon noted, "I'm not too sure about that... I only know that in nine out of every ten cases I hear the same report, 'Dolly just fell down and broke her arm, or broke her nose, or wherever the break might be.' This surely looks as though the falling sickness."

The reporter then offered a "horribly battered" doll to the medical staff. "One eye was entirely gone, and the other had been so viciously jabbed by some sharp weapon that it lay all askew in its scratched orbit. Her nose, at no time a very pronounced feature, had been battered down to a level with her face. Her scalp had been lifted as cleanly as though the job had been done by a Comanche, and the whole of the gray matter lay exposed. One arm had been wrenched out at the shoulder, and her left leg was so shrunken that the skin flapped like an empty football. Yet the poor thing uttered no word of complaint, but lay quietly on her back when the doctor put her down, staring crookedly up at the ceiling with her solitary optic."

The doctor shook his head and noted the doll was another female patient. "I see very few male patients," the attendant noted, then expanded on his observation, reflecting on the effect of mass production of dolls. "The proportion of male to female dolls that have so far come under my observation is about one to a thousand, yet the number of dolls is constantly increasing. In fact, the number is increasing so rapidly and the market value so diminishing that owners are beginning to think that it is almost as cheap to get a new doll as to have a sick one treated. Still, as you see, all the wards are full, and I shall not possibly be able to discharge the patient you have brought me until next Tuesday. The cost of treatment, including a new eye and clinical attendance, will be fifty cents. Good day, sir."

Doll play also reflected the cultural realities of the time as captured in various exchanges reported in frontier newspapers. The *Capital-Journal* in 1892 Salem, Oregon, reported, "Two little girls were playing keep house when a dispute arose as to who should be the wife, both wishing that part. After some discussion, Bessie was heard to explain, 'but you see, you must be the husband 'cause you're the biggest and the bigger you are, the husbander you are'." The *Gazette* in 1893 Shiner, Texas, reported on this interaction: "*Lady*—Where did you get this pretty doll? *Little Girl*—I forgot the name of the place, but it's that great big store where everyone is in a hurry except the ones that make change."

An 1887 ad in the *Oregonian* promoted the doll merchandise of the Golden Rule Bazaar, Cohen, Davis, and Company. "These Dolls are, without a single exception, our direct importations from France, Germany, and England, the home of the doll-makers. They have come to us direct through the Portland Custom House, the duty being paid here and going to swell our city's custom receipts. In buying from us, you practically purchase from the European manufacturer. The goods have been unpacked only once since leaving his hands."

Because of the status appeal of foreign-made dolls—especially those from Paris—to girls and, more likely, their mothers, newspapers ran stories about their manufacture. A Paris correspondent of the *St. Louis Republican* wrote in 1887 about Parisian dolls, stating, "Doll worship has become a sort of creed, and every year these puppets are more expensively and extravagantly dressed. There is no article of woman's attire which is not reproduced in miniature on these aristocratic dolls. There are dolls *deluxe,* which range from three-and-a-half inches to as many feet in height. They wear silk dresses, bustles, long trains, and sealskin dolmans. Their hats take all the fantastic forms of women's and are trimmed with feathers and little tomtits. They wear silk hose, and their feet are encased in dainty satin shoes. There is indeed nothing in the way of eccentricity of dress or foible of millinery which the doll does not wear. Dolls have their own dressmakers, their own milliners, and shoemakers."

The reporter noted that "the aristocratic doll" of the day is made in Paris with hundreds of thousands exported annually, each selling from a half dollar up to four hundred dollars. Their bodies are made from molded paper pulp with elastic bands inserted in the arms, legs, and torso to hold the toy together. After the limbs and torsos are shaped and dried, they get five coats of paint and then one of varnish.

The paper pulp was first worked into a fine mortar. Then the dolls were molded bit by bit. One workman would mold nothing but arms, another the feet, and so on. When the trunks and limbs were shaped and dried, they were painted. The head was molded from porcelain and baked in an oven for twenty-seven hours and then painted.

"The painting and coloring of a doll's head is a ticklish business, requiring, as the French say, the utmost *delicatessen*," the correspondent noted. The doll's eyes were made the same as artificial human eyes, and the hair came from the wool of wild mountain goats from Tibet. "To turn out one of these dolls, thirty different persons are required, and the cheapest is sold naked at sixty cents, and the dearest at eleven dollars."

The 1889 *Bridgeport Chronicle-Union* in Mammoth Lakes, California, reported that nine-tenths of the dolls sold in America come from Germany, especially in Sonneberg, where labor costs are especially cheap. Noted the account, "Before it is completed a doll passes through many hands. The heads, hands, and feet are made by one person; the body by another; the hair is fixed on by another; and the face is painted by two other different people, one doing the rough work and the second the finishing touches. The clothing is made by another person, and the dresses are put on by still another. All this labor is done at such starvation prices that Americans cannot compete in the manufacture, although the duty for importation is thirty-five percent."

Continued the article, "There are at least five hundred different kinds of dolls, and the variety is remarkable. The French invent many of the most attractive, but the Germans copy them so cheaply that the world's buyers go to the latter for their stock. For the manufacture of fine dress dolls, the French still hold the lead by long odds. It is only in the cheaper goods that the Germans out-speed them ... The price of dolls ranges from one cent to fifty dollars, but the most popular are those that sell for twenty-five cents, fifty cents and one dollar, although there has been a great run recently on five-cent and ten-cent dolls."

With such a variety of dolls, public shows or displays originated in England, then crossed the Atlantic to major

U.S. cities and spread across the West. On the frontier, doll shows or fairs were often organized in December so locals could purchase gifts for their daughters and at the same time benefit a local orphanage or church.

In reporting on its inaugural doll show in 1891, the *Capital-Journal* in Topeka, Kansas, noted the American shows originated in Boston and Washington several years earlier and claimed Topeka would be the "first small city to attempt this metropolitan fad." The Topeka show at the fairgrounds was to benefit the local orphans' home. The newspaper, though, had one concern with the arrangement "to give the doll show in connection with the annual state poultry show in the Hentig building." Commented the newspaper, "Chickens and dolls don't go together. The poultry show, instead of being a help to the doll show, will be an injury to it; the odor and the surroundings of a poultry show are not particularly pleasant; the doll show ought to be 'lifted to a higher plane'."

A week later, the paper reported on opening night: "There was a perfect jam of ladies, children, men, and boys at the doll show," which had been moved to another building. "The crowd was larger than anyone had anticipated. Many people were turned away, and some who managed to get inside the door left their breath outside. There was no room to draw it in that crowd." Several hundred dolls were displayed, with many of them sold to the visitors.

In 1886, San Diego, California, hosted a doll show with over two hundred dolls on display. One booth contained a collection of thirty-eight dolls, one representing every state in the Union. "The largest and most valuable is 'California'," reported the California newspaper. "Next to the California doll, the New York representative is the prettiest," concluded the news account.

For San Francisco's annual model doll show at the elegant Palace Hotel in 1898, the *Examiner* reported "There is not a dressmaker of any prominence in the city and Oakland who is not engaged in dressing one or more dolls for the show and the exhibit will be larger than that of last year."

As early as 1878, Waco, Texas, hosted a doll fair to benefit the local orphanage. According to Waco Doll's Fair Association President Lula Gardner, "The little old woman that lives in a shoe has promised to come and bring her numerous family. She even offers to sell, at a good price, some members of her burdensome household, for the benefit of the orphans. Is not that generous?" The association offered prizes for children dressing their dolls and entering them in the beauty contest. Entry fees ranged from fifteen to twenty-five cents. The planners also had a sales table of clothing and fancy articles for dolls and another table of "nicely dressed dolls for sale." Admission was a dime for children and twenty cents for those over sixteen.

The Ladies' Aid Society of the First Baptist Church in Canon City, Colorado, hosted a doll fair, featuring "a grand display of one hundred dolls, ranging in price from five cents to fifteen dollars." Promoters said attending little girls will see "dolls which will cry for her and dolls which will make her cry" and recommended that "everybody should see this troop of dolls before making holiday purchases." The local newspaper reported the following week that the doll's fair "was a financial success" and raised gross receipts of more than five hundred and thirty dollars.

One of the most elaborate doll shows in the West outside of the major metropolitan cities occurred in 1894 in Helena, Montana, with both a doll display and an adapted performance of the German stage production "*Die*

Puppenfee," a ballet in which dolls come to life. The German title translates to "The Fairy Doll." In this Montana production, local residents performed as giant dolls, which sprang to life in an English doll store. Performed two consecutive nights *"Puppenfee,"* as the newspaper described it, drew capacity crowds both performances in Helena's French Renaissance-style auditorium with a floor and gallery seating capacity of two thousand.

The performers represented a singing doll, a dancing doll, a Dutch doll, a "Topsy doll" that played a banjo, a whistling doll, a walking doll, a flower doll, and a talking doll that said "ma-ma" and "pa-pa," according to which string was yanked.

Reported the *Helena Evening Herald*, "Such a crowd of society people as assembled at the Auditorium last evening to attend the doll show and witness the pantomime, *Puppenfee*, has rarely been seen in Helena. The seats, which occupied about half the floor, were all filled, and in many places, standing room was at a premium, while in the gallery several tiers of seats were crowded with the eager spectators."

Such was the appeal of dolls that they could fill a major auditorium in a rugged western town. The appeal was something that lasted in women long after their childhoods had evaporated in the mists of time. The *Daily Independent* in 1890 Elko, Nevada, reprinted a story from *Youth's Companion*, about two wealthy and philanthropic sisters who returned to visit a distant but less prosperous relative who lived in the home of their youth.

Intimidated by the siblings' subsequent wealth and power, their host at first worried about welcoming them back to their childhood home. Their hostess then said, "But I got well over my fear the second day after they came. What do you suppose they did? They went up in the attic, where their old playthings were stored, and unpacked their dolls' clothes. Then they took the little undergarments down into the kitchen, washed them and spread them on the grass to whiten.

"After that they did them up carefully and packed them away again with sprigs of lavender in the little trunk. 'We can't bear to have them grow yellow,' said Miss Martha to me. 'We were so fond of our dolls, and we did have such a fine time making those clothes! Mother's stitches are in them, too'."

In another anecdote related in the Elko paper, a girl of seventeen was busily sewing on a child's dress when a school friend approached and inquired why she was making an outfit too small to wear herself. "It's for the Orphans' Home," she explained. "Don't praise me. I am not doing it for charity. I simply can't forget my play with dolls, and now that I have packed my little family away, for very shame, I want to amuse myself by making clothes for dolls of flesh and blood."

The *Daily Independent* article ended with the tale of a middle-aged woman who adopted a small child. One day a friend, prone to look on the melancholy side of life, asked the adoptive mother if she expected in time to enjoy her new daughter.

"Expect!" cried she; "why, the very first time I took her in my arms, I felt as if Mehitable Arabella, my old rag doll, had come to life. I haven't had such a happy minute in thirty years."

Such was the impact of dolls and toys. They provided memories that lasted a lifetime and memories that shaped the person who sprang from childhood on the American frontier. As adults, those people shaped the course of the growing nation in the coming decades.

Chapter Ten

Pintsized Play

While play is an important element of development in children, it is seldom examined in studies of the West, just as the children themselves are often ignored as well. However, the children were there, thousands of them, from the trek westward on the various trails of the time until the closing of the frontier by the start of the twentieth century. In compiling *Pintsized Pioneers at Play: Homemade Frontier Fun and Danger*, the authors attempted to balance out the work-life portrayal offered in *Pintsized Pioneers: Taming the Frontier, One Chore at a Time* by examining their recreation as well. The authors broadened the definition of recreation or play to cover everything outside of their chores to provide an expanded picture of their childhood experience on the frontier. Consequently, this study also looked at their intellectual development through schooling and their spiritual development through their church and religion.

Whether it was traditional play or the wider definition of everything but work, Old West recreation changed the youngsters and, in many cases, the country itself. For instance, the regular Sunday school and religious services attended by the six Eisenhower brothers in Abilene, Kansas, after the cattle-drive era instilled in them the importance of faith in God and humility in life. Dwight D. Eisenhower, the third of that sibling sextet, believed in those values so much that when he was elected the Thirty-fourth President of the United States in 1952, he soon recommended the words "Under God" be added to the U.S. Pledge of Allegiance. On Flag Day, which fell on June 14 in 1954, President Eisenhower signed a joint resolution of Congress incorporating those words in the national Pledge of Allegiance. The signing date came a week and a day after the tenth anniversary of the D-Day landings, which Eisenhower commanded in Normandy during World War II. His faith had helped him get through those trying times a decade earlier and bring the war in Europe to a close.

Like Eisenhower, Frank Waugh was born elsewhere but arrived in Kansas at age four with his family. Nature fascinated him, so he kept a journal describing the flora and fauna he found around him. Deep down, Waugh never understood his parents' and his neighbors' lack of interest in their natural environment as they plowed up the native plants for farmland and destroyed the habitats of indigenous mammals, birds, reptiles, and insects. Likewise, young Waugh never outgrew his fascination with the natural environment and became a pioneering American landscape architect. His love of the natural environment anchored his influential career that still touches Americans to this day in the development of national forests for recreational use through the U.S. Forest Service. Waugh played an integral role in national forest design and improvement through such projects as the Bryce Canyon Scenic Roadway and the Mount Hood Scenic Byway.

Another young Kansas boy who learned life's lessons from childhood play was William Allen White, who as a child made his own toys, ranging from stick horses to whistles and from wagons to a tiny railroad with whittled ties. Those lessons in self-reliance and ingenuity helped him establish an influential journalism career that began in 1896 when he bought the *Emporia Gazette* and continued until his 1944 death. A 1923 editorial in his paper earned him a Pulitzer Prize. Further, his progressive values and his articulate skill with the written and spoken word garnered him recognition as the voice of Middle America in the first half of the twentieth century.

Though her Nebraska childhood was complicated because of a violent and domineering father who disapproved of her reading books as a child and writing as an adult, Mari Sandoz made the best of an intolerable situation. She played with passing indigenous children when she was never allowed to visit other neighboring farm families. In exchanges with her Sioux playmates, she came to appreciate and value the Plains Indian culture almost as much as she loved to read and write.

Approaching forty years of age in 1935, she published *Old Jules*, a biography of her abusive father and her first major writing success. Her childhood play with her Sioux peers paid off in 1942 with the publication of her monumental biography *Crazy Horse: The Strange Man of the Oglalas*. She wrote her account of the Lakota leader from the Indian viewpoint, using tribe concepts, metaphors, and Lakota speech patterns. She hoped "to say some of the things of the Indian for which there are no white-man words, suggest something of his innate nature, something of his relationship to the earth and the sky and all that is between."

Sandoz was ahead of her time in chronicling the Native American experience and would produce three other works—*Cheyenne Autumn*, *The Horsecatcher*, and *The Story Catcher*—which confirmed her admiration of the Plains Indian culture gained through her play with Sioux children in her youth. She would later be inducted into the Nebraska Hall of Fame, as would Willa Cather.

Though born in Virginia, Cather at the age of nine moved to Nebraska with her family. An astute observer of Nebraska life and an avid reader, Cather loved the traveling theatrical troupes that brought a modicum of culture to Red Cloud, Nebraska. At twelve, she saw her first play, and after that she took in as many as her parents and her allowance would permit. The stage productions, along with her avid reading regimen, further stoked her interest in creative writing.

Though she lived in Nebraska just fourteen years before moving back east to take writing jobs in Pittsburgh, Washington, D.C., and New York City, her girlhood experiences and reminiscences of her years in Nebraska shaped her writing career with many of her early works—*O Pioneers!*, *The Song of the Lark*, and *My Ántonia*—focused on the pioneer experience in Nebraska.

Published in 1927, Cather's *Death Comes for the Archbishop* sold more than eighty-six thousand copies in its first two years on the market. The novel, considered by many critics to be her best, explores the efforts of a Catholic bishop and a priest to establish a diocese in lawless New Mexico Territory in the late nineteenth century. The novel's acclaim earned it inclusion in the Modern Library's One Hundred Best Novels of the Twentieth Century.

Though born in 1882 in New York City, Fiorello Henry La Guardia as the son of a U.S. Army musician, spent his formative years on military posts west of the Mississippi River, starting in Arizona at Fort Huachuca. The experience was paradise for boys, being able to ride and explore the great outdoors without the constraints of the big city. It was grand fun, but not everything La Guardia saw was as appealing because he was a sensitive child with a strong sense of right and wrong. He would return to New York and one day become the city's mayor. His childhood out west shaped his view of politicians and their role in government.

"What I saw and heard and learned in my boyhood days in Arizona made lasting impressions on me," La Guardia noted in his memoirs. "Many of the things on which I have such strong feelings—feelings which some of my opponents have regarded as unreasonable obsessions— were first impressed on my mind during those early days, and the knowledge I acquired then never left me. On some of those things, I believe I am so right in my attitude that I remain uncompromising.

"For instance, there is the professional politician. Though I have been in politics for well over forty years, I loathe the professional politician. I have never been a regular. I have fought political machines and party politics at every opportunity. This attitude had its origin in the loudly dressed, slick, and sly Indian agents—political appointees—I saw come into Arizona.

"The first time I ever heard the word politician was at Fort Huachuca, when I was still a small child. The word was applied to those Indian agents. I learned afterwards that they got the jobs because they were small-fry ward heelers. I saw hungry Indians, and the little Indian kids watch us while we munched a Kansas apple or ate a cookie Mother baked. I knew, even as a child, that the government in Washington provided food for all those Indians, but that the 'politicians' sold the rations to miners and even to general stores, robbing the Indians of the food the government provided for them. That was my first contact with "politicians."

Such observations left a squalid scar on his sense of righteousness, so when he entered politics, first as a New York City alderman, then as a Congressman and finally as mayor he stood up for the little guys and gals and fought corruption at every level. He served as New York's mayor for twelve years, ending in 1946, with a focus on efficient and honest government and on serving even the poorest of his constituents. New York's LaGuardia Airport was named in his honor in 1947. In 1993, a panel of scholars and historians headed by a University of Illinois at Chicago professor ranked La Guardia as the best big-city mayor in American history up to that time.

The American West shaped the outlook of these youngsters early in life and helped them succeed in life, just as they had in play, provided they survived the dangers of the West during their recreation. In the end, the playful spirit of frontier children did more than pass the time on the wide-open plains, in the streets of mining towns, and on the vast lands ranched and cultivated by their parents. It forged the very character of a nation. Through playing games of annie-over around their homes and barns, through making their own toys out of whatever was handy, and through navigating the hazards of frontier play, these pintsized pioneers learned courage, resilience, and quick thinking. Unstructured play honed problem-solving skills, cultivated imagination, and, perhaps most importantly, instilled a communal ethic of fair play and grit.

These children would become the farmers, merchants, teachers, writers, ranchers, mechanics, lawmakers, and parents who built America, carrying forward the lessons learned building toy wagons or fashioning dolls from cornhusks. Their playful inventiveness laid the groundwork for the resourcefulness that defined American progress, while their informal games mirrored the give-and-take needed for democracy to flourish.

In many ways, the laughter of pintsized pioneers at play echoes through time, shaping a uniquely American optimism and can-do spirit. For in the rough-and-tumble joy of the frontier youth, we see the roots of a nation ever eager to dream, build, and push beyond the horizon, always with a playful eye toward the future.

Acknowledgements

This book was written to flesh out the picture of the childhood experience on the American frontier as first portrayed in *Pintsized Pioneers: Taming the Frontier, One Chore at a Time*. That book examined the work life of frontier boys and girls. *Pintsized Pioneers at Play: Homemade Frontier Fun and Danger* explored their leisure time. Both were written for young adults to show them the contributions of their adolescent forebears in settling the American West, through both their labor and their leisure, and in contributing to the nation's greatness.

We would like to think that we are pioneers in studying the role of adolescents on the frontier. We are not. Though we may have been among the first to address the topic for a young adult audience, we relied on the published works of the true pioneers in the field. First among them is Elliott West. *His Growing Up with the Country: Childhood on the Far Western Frontier* was the seminal work in the field, providing an expansive look at the role of boys and girls in the American West. To our knowledge, his 1989 work was the first major work by a professional historian on the topic and more than a quarter of a century later remains a pivotal work. As with all of Dr. West's books, it is insightful and written with a flair that demonstrates his talent as both a historian and a writer.

While Dr. West provided the most substantial treatment of pioneer children throughout the west, several others offered enlightening regional studies. These scholars and their works include Marilyn Irvin Holt, *Children of the Western Plains:*

The Nineteenth-Century Experience; Linda Peavy and Ursula Smith, *Frontier Children*; Elizabeth Hampsten, *Settlers' Children: Growing Up on the Great Plains*; and Craig Miner, *West of Wichita: Settling the High Plains of Kansas, 1865-1890*. Multiple books by Cathy Luchetti were also helpful in this process.

The classic works of some early historians of the American West also offered valuable insights. These included *The Great Plains* by Walter Prescott Webb; *The Sod-House Frontier, 1854-1890* by Everett Dick; and *The Trail Drivers of Texas* by J. Marvin Hunter. Also helpful were *Son of the Old West: The Odyssey of Charlie Siringo: Cowboy, Detective, Writer of the Wild Frontier* by Nathan Ward; *Texas Cowboys: Memories of the Early Days*, edited by Jim Lanning and Judy Lanning; and *Exploring the History of Childhood and Play through 50 Historic Treasures* by Susan A. Fletcher. Useful books from the period included *The American Boys Handy Book* by D.C. Beard and *The American Girls Handy Book* by Lina Beard and Adelia B. Beard.

Memoirs of several pioneers about their childhoods on the frontier were also instructive. Those reminiscences were written by John Taylor Waldorf, David G. Siceloff, Edwin Lewis Bennett, Hamlin Garland, Frances Bramlette Farris, Lily Klasner, and Sarah Harkey Hall. All of these and other authors whose works were beneficial in the writing of this book are listed in the bibliography.

Over the years our love of the history of the Old West and our passion for writing about it have been supported by our membership and participation in Western Writers of America, as caring and supportive an organization as you will ever find devoted to writing. Some members stand out for their support in our efforts and their friendship. The late Jeanne Williams and the late Elmer Kelton, giants in the field of Western writing, served as writing mentors early in our careers. No writer has been more supporting later in our careers than Chris Enss, a talented writer as demonstrated by her *New York Times* bestselling author credentials. She also excels at marketing both of her books and as executive director of the Will Rogers Medallion Awards.

Two writing couples also deserve acknowledgement. Fellow Texas residents Mike and Beverly Cox have been longtime friends. We may not agree on everything, but we have fun and laughs even over our differences. Tom and Marilyn Clagett, our New Mexico neighbors, are a delightful and fun couple with great insights into writing and life. We enjoy our monthly phone conversations and the times we can get together in person for dinner.

This book would not have been possible without the fifty-year partnership of the co-authors. That relationship has not only produced books, but also a son and a daughter. Raising Scott and Melissa was the true joy of our young married lives. The addition of Celeste, our daughter-in-law, enhanced our family and our fun. The subsequent arrival of our grandchildren Hannah, Cora, Miriam, Carys, and Jackson made our family complete. Through them all, we have been truly blessed.

Working on this project together has truly been a blessing for us both. We hope that young readers of *Pintsized Pioneers at Play* will find passages that speak to them and provide insights they can apply to their own lives and ultimately to their future children.

Preston Lewis
 and
Harriet Kocher Lewis
San Angelo, Texas
July 29, 2025

Glossary

Allegorical: an adjective that describes a story, image, or artwork that uses symbolic figures, events, or settings to convey a deeper meaning, often about moral, political, or spiritual truths.

Bisque: In doll making, a doll that is made partially or wholly out of bisque or biscuit porcelain, typically unglazed and characterized by a realistic, skin-like matte finish. Bisque dolls were largely made in France and Germany from the late nineteenth century to the early twentieth century.

Caparison: an ornamental covering for a horse

Centrifugal Force: an apparent force felt by an object moving in a circular or curved path that pushes outward from the center of rotation.

Coal Oil: a flammable liquid obtained from the distillation of bituminous coal, often used for lamp illumination in the nineteenth century

Corporal Punishment: a type of discipline where a paddling or spanking is used to correct someone, usually a child, and shape future behavior

Dolman: a loose outer garment with wide sleeves

Emetic: an agent that induces vomiting

Fain: willingly and gladly

Flies: a theatrical term for the area above a theater stage where scenery, curtains, and sometimes lights are hung and can be raised or lowered out of sight

Gambol: to frolic or skip about in play

Garret: a room or unfinished part of a house just beneath the roof

Great Plains: a North American expanse of flat prairie and grassland, extending from Canada south to Texas and bordered on the east by the hundredth meridian and on the west by the Rocky Mountains

Industrial Revolution: a global transitional period from agrarian-based economies toward large-scale manufacturing societies, beginning in Great Britain around 1760 and spreading to Europe, the United States and elsewhere. The first Industrial Revolution was marked by manufacturing processes using water and steam power with an emphasis on iron-making and machine tooling. The second Industrial Revolution began around 1850 and was characterized by steel-making and the transition to petroleum and electrical sources of energy.

Kerosene: a flammable liquid distilled from petroleum and used for frontier illumination among other things

Lamming: to administer a thorough beating or thrashing or to make a hasty escape or flight

Lath: a thin strip of wood or other building material

Lyceum: a hall for public lectures or an association sponsoring public lectures, concerts and educational programs

Necrosis: localized death of living tissue

Nomenclature: name, designation or terms used to describe something

Muntin: a strip of wood or metal separating panes of glass in a sash

Papeterie: a French word that refers to packaged fancy stationery or a box, often ornamental, for holding stationery

Quirt: a riding whip or rawhide lash

Rabies: an acute viral disease that attacks the nervous system of mammals and is transmitted by animal bites, resulting in abnormal behavior, paralysis and eventual death if left untreated.

Tableau: a striking artistic representation of a scene or group of people arranged to look like a picture or a moment frozen in time

Toggery: clothing, attire

Tomtits: any of several small, active birds with feathers used in doll-making

Tow Sack: a large sack or bag traditionally made of burlap; also called a gunnysack

Sagacity: having keen insight, good judgment, and the ability to understand things deeply and wisely

Vouchsafe: to reveal or disclose; to offer a reply

Ward Heeler: term for an American urban political operative who works for a political party in a political ward to achieve an election result, often by corrupt means

Zephyr: a breeze from the west

Bibliography

For Further Reading

A Kid on the Comstock: Reminiscences of a Virginia City Childhood by John Taylor Waldorf (University of Nevada Press, Reno, 1970)

Boom Town Boy in Old Creede Colorado by Edwin Lewis Bennett and Agnes Wright Spring (Sage Books, Chicago, 1966)

Boy Life on the Prairie by Hamlin Garland (Bison Books, University of Nebraska Press, 1899 & 1961)

Boy Settler in the Cherokee Strip by David G. Siceloff (Caxton Printers, Ltd., Caldwell, Idaho, 1964)

Cat Tales of the Old West: Poems, Puns & Perspectives on Frontier Felines by Preston Lewis (Bariso Press, San Angelo, Texas, 2021)

Children at Play: An American History by Howard P. Chudacoff (New York University Press, New York, London, 2007)

Children of the West: Family Life on the Frontier by Cathy Luchetti (W.W. Norton & Co., New York, 2001)

Children of the Western Plains: The Nineteenth-Century Experience by Marilyn Irvin Holt (Irvin R. Dee, Chicago, 2003)

Everyday Life in the 1800s by Marc McCutcheon (Writer's Digest Books, Cincinnati, 1992)

Exploring the History of Childhood and Play through 50 Historic Treasures by Susan A. Fletcher (Rowman & Littlefield, Lanham, Maryland, 2020)

From Rattlesnakes to Road Agents: Rough Times on the Frio by Frances Bramlette Farris, edited by C.L. Sonnichsen (TCU Press, Fort Worth, 1985)

Frontier Children by Linda Peavy and Ursula Smith (University of Oklahoma Press, Norman, 1999)

Glittering Misery: Dependents of the Indian Fighting Army by Patricia Y. Stallard (University of Oklahoma Press, Norman, 1978)

Growing Up with the Country: Childhood on the Far Western Frontier by Elliott West (University of New Mexico Press, Albuquerque, 1989)

Montgomery Ward & Co. Fall & Winter 1894-95 Catalogue & Buyers Guide No. 56, edited by Joseph J. Schroeder Jr. (Gun Digest Reprint, 1970)

My Childhood Among Outlaws by Lily Klasner, edited by Eve Ball (University of Arizona Press, Tucson, 1972)

Nothing but Prairie and Sky: Life on the Dakota Range in the Early Days by Walker D. Wyman (University of Oklahoma Press, Norman, 1954)

Pioneer Children on the Journey West by Emmy E. Werner (Westview Press, Boulder, Colorado, 1995)

Pioneer Women: Voices from the Kansas Frontier by Joanna L. Stratton (Simon and Schuster, New York, 1981)

Surviving on the Texas Frontier: The Journal of an Orphan Girl in San Saba County by Sarah Harkey Hall (Eakin Press, Austin, 1996)

Settlers' Children: Growing Up on the Great Plains by Elizabeth Hampsten (University of Oklahoma Press, Norman, 1991)

Small Worlds: Children & Adolescents in America, 1850-1950, by Elliott West and Paula Petrik, editors (University of Kansas Press, Lawrence, 1992)

Sod Busting: How Families Made Farms on the Nineteeth-Century Plains by David B. Danbom (John Hopkins University Press, Baltimore, 2014)

So Much to Be Done: Women Settlers on the Mining and Ranching Frontier by Ruth B. Moynihan, Susan Armitage and Christiane Fischer Dichamp, editors (University of Nebraska Press, Lincoln, 1990)

Son of the Old West: The Odyssey of Charlie Siringo: Cowboy, Detective, Writer of the Wild Frontier by Nathan Ward (Atlantic Monthly Press, New York, 2023)

Texas Cowboys: Memories of the Early Days by Jim Lanning and Judy Lanning, editors (Texas A&M University Press, College Station, 1984)

The American Boys Handy Book by D.C. Beard (Charles Scribner's Sons, New York, 1882)

The American Girls Handy Book by Lina Beard and Adelia B. Beard (Charles Scribner's Sons, New York, 1887)

The Bonanza West: The Story of the Western Mining Rushes, 1848-1900 by William S. Greever (University of Oklahoma Press, Norman, 1963)

The Great Plains by Walter Prescott Webb (Grosset & Dunlap, New York, 1931)

The Quirt and the Spur: Vanishing Shadows of the Texas Frontier by Edgar Rye (Texas Tech University Press, Lubbock, 2000)

The Sod-House Frontier, 1854-1890, by Everett Dick (University of Nebraska Press, Lincoln, 1937 & 1954)

The Trail Drivers of Texas by J. Marvin Hunter (University of Texas Press, Austin, 1985)

West of Wichita: Settling the High Plains of Kansas, 1865-1890 by Craig Miner (University of Kansas Press, Lawrence, 1986)

Women of the West by Cathy Luchetti (W.W. Norton & Co., New York, 1982)

About the Authors

Preston and Harriet Lewis have been a team for more than fifty years since they first met and married at Baylor University. Preston has earned multiple national awards for his fiction and nonfiction while Harriet is an award-winning writer and editor with their Bariso Press.

A journalist by training, Preston has published some sixty fiction and nonfiction works on the American West. Western Writers of America (WWA) has honored Lewis with three Spur Awards. The native Texan is the recipient of eleven Will Rogers Medallion Awards (WRMA), including seven gold medallions for western humor, short stories, young adult nonfiction and traditional Westerns.

In 2025 he was named recipient of the WRMA's Lifetime Achievement Award for his contributions to the literature of the American West. In 2021 he was inducted into the Texas Institute of Letters for his literary accomplishments. Preston is a past president of WWA and the West Texas Historical Association, which named him a fellow in 2016.

Harriet Kocher Lewis is editor and publisher of Bariso Press. Titles she has edited have been honored with multiple Will Rogers Medallion Awards, a Spur Award, and multiple Independent Author Awards. In 2025 she received a Spur Award as co-author with her husband of

Pintsized Pioneers: Taming the Frontier, One Chore at a Time.

A native Pennsylvanian, Harriet spent her professional career as a physical therapist, first in clinical settings and then in an academic environment. At Angelo State she taught medical documentation and wrote and edited numerous scientific papers as well as a chapter in a clinical education textbook. She is co-author with Preston of three books in the Magic Machine Series published by Bariso Press.

Harriet holds a bachelor's degree from Baylor University in biology, a physical therapy certificate from the University of Texas Southwestern Medical School, and a master's degree from Texas Tech in kinesiology. Preston holds a bachelor's degree from Baylor and a master's degree from Ohio State University, both in journalism. He earned a second master's degree in history from Angelo State University.

They are parents of a son and a daughter and grandparents of four girls and a boy. They reside in San Angelo, Texas.

Website: barisopress.com
E-mail: barisopress@gmail.com
Facebook: prestonlewisauthor
Website: prestonlewisauthor.com